THE ELEMENTS OF
SOCIAL SCIENTIFIC
THINKING

THE ELEMENTS OF SOCIAL SCIENTIFIC THINKING Third Edition

KENNETH R. HOOVER
The University of Wisconsin–Parkside

St. Martin's Press   New York

Library of Congress Catalog Card Number: 83–61607
Copyright © 1984 by St. Martin's Press, Inc.
All Rights Reserved.
Manufactured in the United States of America.
87654
fedcba
For information, write St. Martin's Press, Inc.,
175 Fifth Avenue, New York, N.Y. 10010

cloth ISBN: 0-312-24188-7
paper ISBN: 0-312-24189-5

Cover painting: The Solomon R. Guggenheim Museum, New York,
Laszlo Moholy-Nagy: AII, 1924.

For
Lee Armstrong Hoover and Margaret Whitcomb Hoover
with memories of wisdom and love

PREFACE

This little book is not very complicated. It is, rather, an initiation to social science intended for those who use the results of social science research and for those taking their first steps as researchers. Where do concepts come from? What is a variable? Why bother with scientific thinking? How is a hypothesis different from other statements about reality? How is it similar? These and other fundamental questions are dealt with here.

My intent has been to help readers see through some false images of social science, and to say enough to make the first steps in research possible, while leaving to more detailed and specialized sources the elaboration of the technicalities of research operations. Throughout, the emphasis is on reality testing as a process by which we can know what to make of the world. This presentation of science is not a narrow one—I encourage the reader to be scientific in daily thought as well as in the specific application of social scientific methods.

Most books are meant to be read straight through. For many readers, that will be the best approach for this book. However, the reader should be aware that each chapter surveys social scientific thinking at a different level. For that reason, there can be various points of access to the book depending on the reader's needs. The first chapter, "Thinking Scientifically," sets social science in the general context of the ways people try to answer questions about the world around them. Chapter Two, "The Elements of Science," develops the basic outline of the scientific method by discussing concepts, variables, measurements, hypotheses, and theory.

For those faced with the immediate task of doing or understanding research, Chapter Three, entitled "Strategies," may be a good place to begin since it deals directly with the nuts and bolts of scientific inquiry. Chapter Four, "Refinements," presumes a basic understanding of the scientific method explained in Chapter Two and provides additional research tools. Chapter Five is devoted to the art and science of measurement. Chapter Six, "Reflections: Back to the Roots," should be read, I think, by those who use the book for whatever purpose. The point of the concluding chapter is to place scientific understanding in perspective and to suggest generally where humility is advisable and achievement possible.

For convenience of access and review, each chapter begins with an outline of the topics covered and ends with a list of the major concepts introduced, in their order of appearance.

In Appendix A, an article by Professor Lewis Lipsitz of the University of North Carolina, "Work Life and Political Attitudes," is reprinted. The article is cited frequently in the text; those who need a good model for the design and discussion of a research project will want to consider it carefully. In Appendix B, an excerpt is reprinted from the article "Pathways to Participation" by Paul Allen Beck and M. Kent Jennings. This excerpt pertains only to the newly added section on regression and path analysis in Chapter Five.

Changes in the Third Edition

In preparing this edition, we have again asked for the advice of some of those who use this book as a text in university and college classrooms around the country. As with the second edition, a number of helpful suggestions were made, but the unanimous sentiment being for clarity and brevity. This advice has been taken to heart; my objectives have been to add only where essential and to revise strictly in the interest of precision.

The major change involves a new Chapter Five, "Measuring Variables and Relationships." The new chapter begins with the material on measurement previously found in an overlong Chapter Four. Added to this material is a new section on regression analysis. The discussion of regression is aimed more at the consumer than at the practitioner of regression statistics and proposes only to communicate the basic form and uses of regression. The new Appendix B excerpts an article that supplies examples of regression analysis applied to the topic of political participation. The discussion of regression is clearly optional in both the structure and sequencing of topics.

I trust that the many minor revisions of the language and the updating of some references will make the book more readable and instructive.

Acknowledgments

I especially thank those who responded to my request for suggestions for the third edition, as well as the anonymous critics who so carefully reviewed this edition. I have tried to accommodate the spirit, if not always the letter, of these comments and to arbitrate between various conceptions of key issues. In addition, I would also like to thank Franklin Gilliam, Jr., and Sue Strickler, my colleagues at the University of Wisconsin–Parkside, and the students in our research methods course for their interest and assistance.

My list of acknowledgments from the second edition includes some especially helpful colleagues. Bob Blair was a good friend and trusty resource throughout the project. For comments and suggestions at various stages may I again thank Philip Zweifel, Gene Pollock, Frank Miller, Steve Victor, Bradlee Karan, and Gordon Shull. Welcome assistance was provided by the National Science Foundation, the College of Wooster Leave Program, and the Faculty Development Fund.

Aage Clausen of Ohio State University did a particularly thoughtful and meticulous critique of the original manuscript and that of each later edition. Working with Barry Rossinoff, Bob Woodbury, Walter Kossmann, and Patricia Mansfield of St. Martin's Press was a pleasure.

To all of these I am indebted, as are the readers of this book, though neither they nor I may hold them responsible for the result.

Judy Hoover contributed some helpful suggestions in the writing, and a lot more that I couldn't begin to acknowledge. Andrew and Erin appear briefly in the second chapter and are present throughout in the nurture of the spirit they provided to their father.

KENNETH R. HOOVER
University of Wisconsin–Parkside
University of Wisconsin Extension—
Department of Governmental Affairs

The third edition has benefited from the thoughtful comments of:

Gilbert M. Almquist
Brigham Young
   University

James M. Carlson
Providence College

L. H. Nitz
University of Hawaii

Charles R. Green
Macalester College

David Cox
Memphis State University

Brian D. Silver
Michigan State University

Jerold M. Starr
West Virginia University

Larry J. Zimmerman
University of South Dakota

Edward C. Uliassi
Northeastern Illinois
   University

J. Gaines
University of Kentucky

Richard Guarasci
St. Lawrence University

Jerry Maneker
California State University—
   Chico

Bradley Kent Carter
Southern Methodist University

Jack Noragon
Ohio State University—Marion

Thomas J. Pavlak
University of Pittsburgh

Stuart Gilman
St. Louis University

Gary D. Sardefur
University of Oklahoma

xii

CONTENTS

CONTENTS

xiv

THE ELEMENTS OF
SOCIAL SCIENTIFIC
THINKING

OUTLINE

2

CHAPTER ONE

THINKING SCIENTIFICALLY

"Science searches the common experience of people; and it is made by people, and it has their style."

JACOB BRONOWSKI

"Social science" in cold print gives rise to images of some robot in a statistics laboratory reducing human activity to bloodless digits and simplified formulas. Research reports filled with mechanical-sounding words like "empirical," "quantitative," "operational," "inverse," and "correlative" aren't very poetic. Yet the stereotypes of social science created by these images are, I will try to show, wrong.

Like any other mode of knowing, social science can be used for perverse ends; however, it can also be used for humane personal understanding. By testing thoughts against reality, science helps liberate inquiry from bias, prejudice, and just plain muddleheadedness. So it is unwise to be put off by simple stereotypes—too many people accept these stereotypes and deny themselves the power of social scientific understanding.

The word "science" stands for a very great deal in our culture—some even consider it the successor to religion in the modern age. Our objective here is not to examine the whole tangle of issues associated with science; it is to find a path into the scientific way of thinking about things. In order to find that path, we will begin not by defining science but rather by allowing some descriptions of science to emerge out of contrasts with other forms of knowledge.

First, we have to identify some distractions that should be ignored. Science is sometimes confused with technology, which is the application of science to various tasks. Grade-school texts that caption pictures of rockets on the moon with the title, "Science Marches On!" aid such confusion. The technology that makes landings on the moon possible emerged from the use of scientific strategies in the study of propulsion, electronics, and numerous other fields. It is the mode of inquiry that is scientific; the rocket is a piece of technology.

Just as science is not technology, neither is it some specific body of knowledge. The popular phrase *"Science tells us* [for example] that smoking is bad for your health" really misleads. "Science" doesn't tell us anything; people tell us things, in this case people who have used scientific strategies to investigate the relationship of smoking to health. Science, as a way of thought and investigation, is best conceived of as existing not in books, or in machinery, or in reports containing numbers, but rather in that invisible world of the mind. Science has to do with the way questions are formulated and answered; it is a set of rules and forms for inquiry created by people who want reliable answers.

Another distraction comes from identifying particular persons as "scientists." That usage isn't false, since the people so labeled practice the scientific form of inquiry, but neither is it fully honest to say that some people are scientists, whereas others are nonscientists. Science is a mode of inquiry that, we will see shortly, is common to all human beings. Some people specialize in scientific approaches to knowledge, but we are all participants in the scientific way of thinking.

In becoming more self-conscious of your own habits of thought, you will find that there is some science in all of us. We measure, compare, modify beliefs, and acquire a kind of savvy about evidence in the daily business of figuring out what to do next and how to relate to others. The simplest of games involves the testing of tactics and strategies against the data of performance, and that is crudely scientific. Even trying out different styles of dress for their impact on others has an element of science in it.

The scientific way of thought is one of a number of strategies by which we try to cope with a vital reality: the uncertainty of life. We don't know what the consequences of many of our actions will be. We may have

5

little idea of the forces that affect us subtly or directly, gradually or suddenly. In trying to accomplish even the simplest task, like figuring out what to eat, we do elementary calculations of what might taste good or what might be good for us. If there's enough uncertainty on that score, a little advance testing is a good idea: the king has his taster, and the rest of us, at least when it comes to a certain hamburger, have the assurance that billions have already been sold.

The scientific approach has many competitors in the search for understanding. For many people throughout most of history, the competitors have prevailed. Analysis of reality has usually been much less popular than myths, superstitions, and hunches, which have the reassuring feel of certainty *before* the event they try to predict or control, though seldom afterwards. Sometimes unverified belief sponsors an inspired action or sustains the doubtful until a better day. Certainly personal beliefs are a vital part of our lives. The point is that the refusal to analyze is crippling, and the skilled analyst is in a position of strength.

Why Bother to Be Systematic?

Most human communication takes place among small groups of persons who share a common language and much common experience and understanding of the world they live in. There is a ready-made arena for mutual agreement. Not so in a more complex social environment. Though families can transmit wisdom across generations by handing down stories and maxims, societies run into trouble. In its most cynical form, the question is, "Whose story is to be believed?" The need to understand what is happening around us and to share experiences with others makes systematic thought and inquiry essential.

Because society is interesting for the drama it contains, there is a tendency to dispense with systematic understanding and get on with the descriptions, stories, and personal judgments. Although these are illuminating, they often have limited usefulness, because highly subjective accounts of life form a poor basis for the development of common understanding and common action.

The intricate task of getting people to bridge the differences that arise from the singularity of their experience requires a more disciplined approach to knowledge. *Knowledge is socially powerful only if it is knowledge that can be put to use.* Social knowledge, if it is to be useful, must be *communicable, valid,* and *compelling.*

In order to be communicable, knowledge must be in clear form. And if the knowledge is intended to be used as a spur to action, it must be valid in light of the appropriate evidence and compelling in the way that it fits the question raised. A personal opinion like "I think that capitalism exploits the poor" may influence your friends and even your relatives to think that there is some injustice in our society. But it probably won't make any waves with others. If, however, you can cite the evidence that "In our capitalistic system, 10 percent of the people control 50 percent of the wealth, and 50 percent of the people control less than 10 percent of the wealth," a more compelling argument results, because you relate a judgment to a measurement of reality. People who don't even like you, but who favor some kind of fairness in wealth distribution, might find such a statement a powerful cue to examine our economic system critically. Knowledge built on evidence, and captured in clear transmissible form, makes for power over the environment.

Accumulating knowledge so that past mistakes can be avoided has always intrigued civilized humanity. One can record the sayings of wise persons, and that does contribute greatly to cultural enrichment. Yet there is surely room for another kind of cumulative effort: the building up of statements evidenced in a manner that can be double-checked by others. To double-check a statement requires that one know precisely what was claimed and how the claim was tested. This is a major part of the enterprise of science. The steps to be discussed in Chapter Two in the section on the scientific method are the guideposts for accomplishing that kind of knowing.

The Role of Reasoned Judgment and Opinion

All this vaguely ominous talk about systematic thinking is not meant to cast out reasoned judgment, opinion, and imagination. There is no particular sense in limiting the facilities of the mind in any inquiry.

Reasoned judgment is a staple of human understanding. A reasoned judgment bears a respectable relationship to evidence. Because people inevitably have to act in the absence of complete evidence for decision making, the term "judgment" is important. Judgment connotes decision making in which all the powers of the mind are activated to make the best use of available knowledge.

Reasoned judgment is the first part of systematic thought. The proposition that "A full moon on the eve of election day promotes liberal voting" could be correct, but it does not reflect much reasoned judgment, since there is neither evidence for linking the two events nor a logical connection between them. An investigator with time and resources might look into such a proposition, but in a world of scarce time, inadequate resources, and serious problems of social analysis to engage rare talents, such an investigation makes little sense.[1] Although the proposition may be intuitive, even intuition usually bears some relationship to experience and evidence.

Opinion likewise plays an inescapable role in scientific analysis, because all efforts at inquiry proceed from some personal interest or other. No one asks a question unless there is an interest in what the conclusion might be. Furthermore, each person's angle of vision on reality is necessarily slightly different from the angle of another. Opinion can't be eliminated from inquiry, but it can be controlled so that it does not fly off into complete fantasy. One practice that assists in reducing the role of opinion is for the researcher to be self-conscious of his or her values and opinions.

Plato's famous aphorism, "Know thyself," applies

---

[1]However, police and bartenders will tell you that the night of a full moon does in fact bring out some pretty bizarre behavior; the hypothesis isn't completely preposterous.

here more than ever. Much damage has been done to the cause of good social science by those who pretend disinterest to the point where their research conceals opinions that covertly structure their conclusions. No one is truly objective, certainly not about the nature of society—there are too many personal stakes involved for that.

Ultimately, good science provides its own check on the influence of values in an inquiry. If the method by which the study has been done and the evidence for conclusions are clearly and fully stated, the study can be examined for the fit of conclusions to evidence. If there is doubt about the validity of what has been done, the study itself can be double-checked, or "replicated," to use the technical term. This feature distinguishes science from personal judgment.

No one can double-check everything that goes on as the mind deals with inner feelings, perceptions of experience, and thought processes. Science brings the steps of inquiry out of the mind and into public view so that they can be shared as part of the process of accumulating knowledge.

The Role of Imagination, Custom, and Intuition

The mind, in its many ways of knowing, is never so clever or so mysterious as in the exercise of *imagination*. If there is any sense in which people can leap over tall obstacles at a single bound, it is in the flight of the mind. But it is one thing to imagine a possible proposition about reality, and it is quite another to start imagining evidence.

Science is really a matter of figuring out relationships between things we know something about. To propose a relationship is a creative and imaginative act, however much systematic preparation may lie in the background. To test a proposition against reality involves a different order of imagination—mainly the ability to find in the bits and pieces of information elicited from reality that item essential to testing the credibility of a particular idea.

It is in the realm of discovery that science becomes a direct partner of imagination. The history of natural science is filled with examples, from the realization that the earth revolves around the sun, and not vice versa, to the discovery that matter is made up of tiny atoms. Each of these discoveries was made by bold and imaginative people who were not afraid to challenge a whole structure of customary belief by consulting evidence in the real world. While these were discoveries on the grand scale, the same sort of effort is involved in stepping outside accepted explanations of human behavior to imagine other possibilities and test them by the intelligent use of evidence. To be truly imaginative is something like trying to escape gravity—the initial move is the hardest. While the social sciences have as yet few discoveries to compare with the feats of natural science, the application of science to social relations is a much more recent and vastly more complicated undertaking.[2]

---

[2]Perhaps one of the earliest attempts to confront social custom with science was the effort in the late nineteenth century by Francis Galton, an

Whatever we may come to say about the careful thinking scientific analysis requires, there is still no way to capture completely the wondrous process of "having an idea." Science is absolutely *not* a system for frustrating that exercise of intuition and imagination; rather it is a set of procedures for making such ideas as fruitful and productive as human ingenuity allows. Even the most wonderful idea, whatever its source, is only as good as its relationship to some present or potential reality. Science is the art of reality testing, of taking ideas and confronting them with evidence drawn from the phenomena to which they relate.

To step back from the general blur of human relationships and envision alternative possibilities demands a level of imagination that is as uncommon as it is necessary. In the usual run of social and political experience, David Hume's observation may be sadly accurate: "Men, once accustomed to obedience, never think of departing from that path in which they and their ances-

---

English scientist, to test the efficacy of prayer. Observing that prayers were daily offered in churches throughout the land for the long life of royalty, he compared their longevity to that of the gentry and a variety of professionals. He found, after excluding deaths by accident or violence, and including only those who had survived their thirtieth year, that the average age of decease for royalty was 64.04 years, the lowest age for all his categories. Galton did observe, however, that prayer has many personal uses aside from the fulfillment of requests. And, who knows, royalty might have died even sooner but for such petitions. P. B. Medawar, *Induction and Intuition in Scientific Thought* (Philadelphia: American Philosophical Society, 1969), pp. 2–7.

tors trod and to which they are confined by so many urgent and visible motives." [3]

Yet it is in the understanding and reform of social and political arrangements that the world requires the very best application of disciplined imagination. That the world we live in is unsatisfactory in these respects is evidenced by the amount of time spent drilling into the heads of the young patriotic slogans and altruistic maxims that bear little relationship to the reality of the state or the frequency of human benevolence. If our community life could be made more sensible and humane, these rituals would not require so much effort. In the absence of imaginative efforts to understand the reality of society, we are confined to the beaten path of custom and the inequities that stifle human potential.

We may also be confined to some very unproductive habits of behavior. It used to be the custom in England to hang pickpockets publicly in order to discourage others in the trade. Someone noticed, however, that *more* pockets were picked at pickpocket hangings than at other public events. The custom survived that bit of social science far longer than it should have.

Custom is not all bad, for it may embody the lessons learned from a long, often unhappy, experience with reality and is, in a vague way, scientific. Custom frequently holds communities together in the face of

---

[3] "Of the Origin of Government," *Political Essays*, ed. Charles Hendel (New York: Liberal Arts Press, 1953), p. 41.

enormous and even violent pressures. Yet the task of any social science must be to understand why things are the way they are, as well as how the elements of social life can be reformed to allow for more humane patterns of personal development and expression. The weapons in this struggle for understanding are not only science with its procedures for disciplining inquiry, but also the intuition that life can be better than it is, that a given pattern of behavior may be other than inevitable, that even the smallest transactions of behavior may contain the keys to larger structures of possibility and potential.

The method of any effort at understanding involves a tension between thought and investigation. There are various ways of linking these two components. The mystic perceives an inner truth and interprets "signs" that he or she finds in reality as symptoms of the validity of the insight. The historian looks for patterns in the past and, having conceptualized them, suggests their usefulness in interpreting the major features of previous events. Thus the "rise of the middle class" in Europe becomes a major interpretive concept. Someone who is scientific attempts to be more concrete than the mystic and more precise than the historian with respect to the *thoughts* by which research is guided, the *data* regarded as significant in the investigation, and the *measures* used in testing mental constructions against reality.

In the chapters that follow, the steps involved in building scientific understanding will be taken one at a time. As you will see, the technique requires common sense more than technical knowledge or elaborate preparation.

THINKING SCIENTIFICALLY

CONCEPTS INTRODUCED

Science

Technology

Communicable knowledge

Valid knowledge

Compelling knowledge

Reasoned judgment

Opinion

Objectivity

Imagination

Custom

Intuition

OUTLINE

16

CHAPTER TWO

THE ELEMENTS OF SCIENCE

"[Scientific inquiry] begins as a story about a Possible World—a story which we invent and criticize and modify as we go along, so that it ends by being, as nearly as we can make it, a story about real life."

P. B. MEDAWAR

To see scientific thought in the context of other kinds of thinking, as we have tried to do, tells us why we should be interested in science. Now it is time to see what science is made of.

The elements of a scientific strategy are, in them-

17

selves, simple to understand. They are: concepts, variables, hypotheses, and measurements. The way in which these are combined constitutes the scientific method. It is the function of theory to give meaning and motivation to this method by enabling us to interpret what we observe. First, we will try to put each element in place.

The Origin and Utility of Concepts

If you had to purge all words and other symbols from your mind and confront the world with a virgin mind, what would you do? Without a body to sustain, you might do nothing. The necessities of survival, however, start closing in, and the first act of the mind might be to sort out the edible objects from the inedible, then the warm from the cold, the friendly from the hostile. From there it isn't very far to forming concepts like *food, shelter, warmth,* and symbolizing these concepts in the form of words or utterances. Thus, humbly, emerges the instrument called language. The search for truly usable concepts and categories is under way. Languages are nothing more than huge collections of names for things, feelings, and ideas generated by people in the course of relating to each other and to their environment.

Some concepts and classifications might not be very helpful. To conceptualize all plants under only a single designation would preclude further distinctions between those that are edible, those that heal, and those that poison. Some concepts relate to experience too vaguely: English has but one word for something so various and complicated as love. Greek allows three concepts: *eros* for romantic love, *agape* for generalized feelings of affection, and *filios* for family love. The inadequacy of English in dealing with the concept *love* affects everyone's experience through the tricky ways the word is used in our culture.

Notice that reality testing is built right into the process of naming things, one of the most elementary transactions of existence. That back-and-forth between the stimuli of the environment and the reflections of the mind makes up the kind of thought we will be trying to capture for analysis.

After several thousand years of history, we still have to face the fact that the process of naming things is difficult. Language emerges essentially by agreement. You and I and the other members of the family (tribe, state, nation, world) agree, for example, to call things that twinkle in the sky "stars." Unfortunately, these agreements may not be very precise. In common usage, the term "star" covers a multitude of objects, big and small, hot and cold, solid and gaseous.

To call a thing by a precise name is the beginning of understanding, because it is the key to the procedure that allows the mind to grasp reality and its many relationships. It makes a great deal of difference whether an illness is conceived of as caused by the Evil Spirit or by bacteria on a binge. The concept *bacteria* is tied to a system of concepts in which there is a connection to a powerful repertory of treatments, that is, antibiotics.

Old movie serials about jungle tribes and Indians often have an episode featuring a confrontation between the local medicine man and the doctor who triumphs for modern science by saving the chief or his child. The cultural agreement that supported the medicine man is shattered by the scientist with his microscope. Sadly for the children of modern medicine, it turns out that there were a few tricks in the medicine man's bag that were ignored or lost in the euphoria of such a "victory" for science. Even less happy was the arrogance with which many of the cultural agreements expressed in native languages were undermined through the supposition of superiority by conquering powers. To capture meaning in a language is a profound and subtle process, even if it is a little sloppy. While you are invited to be precise about concepts, you are not invited to be arrogant about the utility of your new knowledge for reworking lives, societies, and civilizations.

The importance of having the right name for a thing can hardly be overestimated. Thomas Hobbes, a seventeenth-century political theorist, thought the proper naming of things so important to the establishment of political order that he made this a central function of the sovereign. King James understood the message and ordered an authoritative translation of the Bible as a way of overcoming violent squabbles about the precise meanings of words in the Scripture. More to the modern scene, George Orwell, in his anti-utopian novel, *1984*, gave us a vision of a whole bureaucracy devoted to reconstructing language concepts to enhance the power of a totalitarian society. A recent presidential press secretary made a game try at redefining a lie by calling a previous statement "inoperative." These examples are intended to make you aware that by tinkering with the meanings of concepts, you are playing with the foundations of human understanding and social control.

But it will be a while before you master the scientific method sufficiently to pull off anything very grand. For now, the point is that concepts are: (1) tentative, (2) based on agreement, and (3) useful only to the degree that they capture or isolate some significant and definable item in reality.

What have concepts got to do with science? If you've spent any time around babies, you may notice that they often try to show off by pointing at things and naming them. It gets a little boring the tenth or fifteenth time through, but babies take justifiable pride in the exercise. Next come sentences. From naming things, from being able to symbolize something rather than simply pointing at it, comes the next step in moving reality around so it can produce things that are needed. The first sentence our son Andrew spoke was to his sister Erin. Sitting on a little cart he said, "Erin, push me!" She did.

What you are reading now is an effort to link together concepts in order to expand your understanding. People speak sentences by the thousands in an attempt to move reality into some useful response. Most of them don't have the good luck Andrew did on his first try. Often the concepts are confusing, and the connections are vague or unlikely, not to mention the problem that the speaker has with the listener's perceptions and motives.

Thought develops through the linking of concepts. Consider, as an example, Pierre Proudhon's famous proposition, "Property is theft!" Property, as a concept, stands for the notion that a person can claim sole ownership of land or other resources. Theft, of course, means the act of taking something without justification.

21

By linking these two concepts through the verb "is," Proudhon meant to equate the institution of private property with the denial of humankind's common ownership of nature's resources. The concept of privately owned property was, he thought, unjustifiable thievery. While Proudhon's declaration illustrates the linkage of concepts at the lofty philosophical level, the humblest sentence performs the same operation.

Science is a way of checking on the formulation of concepts and testing the possible linkages between them through references to observable phenomena. The next step is to see how scientists use a special kind of concept, the *variable*, to form a special kind of sentence, the *hypothesis*.

What Is a Variable?

A variable is a name for something that is thought to influence (or to be influenced by) a particular state of being in something else. Heat is one variable in making water boil, and so is pressure. Age has been established as a modestly important variable in voting; however, there are many other more significant variables: socioeconomic standing, parental influence, race, sex, region of residence, and so on.

A variable is, in addition, a special kind of concept that contains within it a notion of degree or differentiation. Temperature is an easily understood example of a variable. It includes the notion of more or less heat. Religion is a variable of a different kind; though there may be such a thing as more or less religion, it is likely that one would look to the several denominations of religion in, for example, assessing voting behavior. In 1968, the Gallup Poll found that a fairly predictable 35 percent of Protestants voted Democratic for president, but an abnormally low 59 percent of Catholics voted for the Democrats' Humphrey. This signaled a defection from the Kennedy–Johnson years when the Catholic percentages were in the high 70s. Evidence such as this permits us to say something intelligent about the relationship between two variables: religion and voting.

While most variables deal with differences of degree, as in temperature, or differences of variety, like religion, some variables are even simpler. These deal with the most elementary kind of variation: present or absent, there or not there, existent or nonexistent. Take pregnancy, for example. There is no such thing as a little bit of it. Either the condition exists or it doesn't.

Variable definition, dull as it may seem, is a very creative process and often raises immense questions. Consider, as an illustration, such an ordinary variable as time. The early Greeks puzzled a good deal over how to conceptualize this variable. It seems obvious that time has to be thought of as having a beginning—so philosophers went about trying to figure out when the beginning was. Yet the nagging question always popped up—What happened before that? Plato and Aristotle both played with the idea that time might not be linear at all, that is, it might *not* have a beginning, a progression, and presumably an end. It just might be cyclical! This seems crazy to us children of linear time, but they were thinking that universal time might be something like the cycle of the body, a rhythm found everywhere in nature. Historic time, therefore, might best be conceived of as an unfolding structure of events

23

in which one follows the other until the whole pattern is played out and the entire cycle starts over again. Aristotle commented that it just might be that he himself "was living *before* the Fall of Troy quite as much as *after* it, since, when the wheel of fortune had turned through another cycle, the Trojan War would be re-enacted and Troy would fall again."[1]

The social science done by introductory students seldom involves such mind-boggling conceptual problems, yet it wouldn't do to pretend that these problems don't exist. The variable *personality,* for example, is reputed to have over four hundred definitions in the professional literature, partly because personality is a compound of a huge range of other variables: class, status, self-concept, race, socialization, and so forth. The complexity of personality as a variable has driven social scientists to such awkward definitions as: "One's acquired, relatively enduring, yet dynamic, unique system of predispositions to psychological and social behavior."[2]

Even when social scientists agree on the description of a variable, that doesn't mean the definition possesses the qualities of eternal truth—it just means that some people who have thought about it carefully agree that a given definition seems to help answer some questions. This is frustrating, but that's all that can be said, except to point out that *not* facing the problem of speci-

[1]Stephen Toulmin and June Goodfield, *The Discovery of Time* (New York: Harper & Row, 1965), p. 46.
[2]Gordon DiRenzo, *Personality and Politics* (Garden City, N.Y.: Anchor Books, 1974), p. 16.

fying variables in analysis doesn't make the problem go away, it just gets you further into the linguistic soup.

The huge stock of concepts in language creates enormous possibilities for linking up variables to explain events. People have muddled around for centuries trying to sort through significant connections. Science is a slightly elevated form of muddling by which these connections are tried out and tested as carefully as possible. In medical science, it took centuries to isolate the many variables affecting disease. Only recently has medical science become so disciplined that it can diagnose many diseases through highly significant blood-chemistry analysis. This development represents the present stage of a long process of isolating and eliminating a host of unimportant or marginally significant variables. Western doctors have just recently come up against an ancient form of medicine developed to a high art in China, and now we have medical scientists scrambling to figure out why acupuncture works. Whole new sets of variables must now be considered and new conceptual bridges built.

Unfortunately for *social* science, we have barely figured out how to lay the foundation for a structure of theory to explain social behavior. Many new students of social science do not see—especially when confronted by fat texts in introductory courses—the context of struggle and accomplishment, tentativeness and probability, behind what has been achieved in social understanding.

Social science currently contains many subdivisions (e.g., political science, sociology, economics, psychology, education), all of which are working on specific variables within subsystems of behavior. Social scien-

25

tists are in the process of chasing a good many possible connections between variables. The bits of tested knowledge that do emerge await an integration across the lines of these inquiries. Relatively few have been attempted, though these efforts are bound to increase in view of the dramatic need for comprehensive social understanding.

Quantification and Measurement: How to Get Inside a Variable

We said earlier that variables are special concepts that contain within them some notion of degree or differentiation. The next question is: How does one pin down that degree or differentiation? The answer involves a two-step process: quantification and measurement.

The idea of *quantification* means setting up a standard amount of a thing and putting a label on it. The origins of some quantifications are pretty weird. The English, for example, needed a standard quantity of distance, so they settled on the length of some king's foot. For a long time, the foot competed with the cubit, which was the length of someone else's forearm. The trouble with the cubit was that they could never agree on what the standard forearm was—some said seventeen inches, some said twenty-one inches. Consequently, we don't hear much about cubits anymore.

Isolating standardized units increases the power of description and analysis. When Gabriel Fahrenheit established the idea of a degree of temperature, he made possible a much more useful description of hot and cold. It makes a considerable difference with respect to

a puddle of water if the temperature is thirty-two degrees rather than thirty-three degrees—the word
"cold" doesn't work very well for capturing that vital
degree of difference.

Quantification in social science takes two forms:
discrete and continuous. Discrete quantification relates
to counting the units of a thing. A vote is a discrete and
specific act that can be counted in a conventional manner. Some quantifications, however, have to capture
the notion of variation along a continuum. Age is an
example of a continuous quantification. True, one can
count the number of years in a person's age, but the
quantification of age is an expression of something that
is ongoing. I am 42.704 years old today; next Monday
I will be 42.715 years old. Continuous quantification
deals not with discrete items, but rather with dimensions like age, length, and time. The mark of continuous
quantification is that the variable involved may have
any value on a scale, whereas in discrete quantification
only whole numbers appear, as in a counting process.

Each variable has its own peculiar problems and
potentials for quantification. One of the distinguishing
characteristics of a well-developed science is the array
of useful quantifiable variables it has developed; one of
the marks of a smart scientist is the ability to find ways
of quantifying important variables in a reliable and
meaningful way. Economics has come a long way by
using money as a unit of analysis. Many powerful economic indicators, such as the gross national product or
the consumer price index, are based on money. Unfortunately for the other social sciences, there aren't such
easily quantifiable units for psychological stress, alienation, happiness, personal security, and so on. Yet inven-

tive scientists have found more or less successful ways of capturing quantifiable pieces of these variables. A text in any of these areas contains dozens of illustrations, and we will see some of them in the next chapter. The importance of quantification is that, when it can be accomplished, there is the potential for more precise measurement.

Measurement is not something we choose to do or not do—it is inherent in every analytic discussion. If you doubt this, listen carefully in the next conversation you have and notice your dependence on terms that imply measurement. A simple political statement such as, "Democrats generally favor the poor," involves measurement. The verb "favor" implies degrees of difference, and so does the term "poor." The modifier "generally" is an attempt to qualify the measurement by indicating that it is not a universal characteristic of all Democrats.

If quantities can be established, measurement becomes much easier. The most obvious measurement deals with the problem of *how much:* how much distance, how much money, and so forth. Some questions of how much are not so easy to measure; public opinion, for example. Using responses to questions as the quantifiable unit of analysis, the most elementary technique divides opinion into favorable versus unfavorable. "Are you for it or against it?" Public-opinion polling is usually done on this basis. One thing such a simple measurement conceals, of course, is the intensity of the opinion. On many political issues there may be minorities that are passionately on one side and a majority that is lukewarmly on the other side. Some public-opinion polls deal with this by using four categories instead of two:

Strongly For   For   Against   Strongly Against

An even fancier way of addressing the problem is to use scales: a scale of 1 to 10, from never-say-die opposition to enthusiastic support. This helps expand the range of responses and reveals more accurately the state of opinion. A political system that simply acts on majority sentiment without taking intensity into account can get itself into a lot of trouble—as this nation did on the Vietnam War. A passionate minority of opponents became embittered and alienated by the reliance of policy makers on a rather unenthusiastic majority of supporters.

Quantified measurement, properly conceived and executed, has the potential for specifying differentiation and degree more effectively than fuzzy words in vague sentences. At the same time, improperly conceived measurement is dangerous precisely because it can be so powerful. A tragic and repugnant example is the use of "body counts" as a key to "progress" in the U.S. effort in Vietnam. Newscasts about the war would usually report the military's figures on how many "enemies" were killed each day. The implication was that the more we killed, the faster we would win the war. There were two things wrong with this quantified measurement. First, it didn't measure what some policy makers alleged that it measured: the amount of success or failure in achieving overall objectives in the war. Since the war was at least as much a political and psychological struggle as a military conflict, the body counts were largely useless as an index of success. They may have told the military something about the condition of the enemy, but reliance on them promoted adverse political and psychological effects in the Vietnamese population and in ours. The Vietnamese began to notice that it was people of their own race and nationality who were being killed by Americans, regardless of whatever else the war was about. Americans came to be feared rather than welcomed as allies by many Vietnamese. At the same time, we began to see ourselves as technological warriors wreaking havoc in a poor country.

A second flaw in the measurement was its implementation. Troops in the field were supposed to count enemy dead and report the number. However, several factors intervened: the confusion (sometimes deliberate) about who was the enemy, the error introduced by having more than one person counting in a particular location, and the chain-of-command pressures for a high body count. Consequently, while the body counts kept going up and led to predictions of success in the war, the actual situation deteriorated.[3]

The very important point is that sloppy or inappropriate measurement is generally worse than no measurement at all. Interpreting the results of measurement requires an understanding of the measurement itself. In Chapter Five, we explore the practical steps involved in making and interpreting measurements.

[3]Body counting as an indicator reached immoral depths with "bounty hunting" in which U.S. Army counterintelligence units hired assassins to kill suspected communist sympathizers—the payments were made by the number of *ears* brought in to headquarters. Where money was involved, the counting was made more specific. Michael Drosnin, *New Times Magazine* 5 (22 August 1975): 16–24.

The Hypothesis

Although much of the preceding discussion may have seemed like a serial review of bits and pieces of scientific thinking, a discussion of hypotheses will bring these matters together.

The purpose of a hypothesis is to organize a study. If the hypothesis is carefully formed, all the steps of the scientific method follow, as does an outline for the project, a bibliography, a list of resources needed, and a specification of the measures appropriate to the study. The hypothesis provides the structure. A hypothesis is a sentence of a particularly well-cultivated breed.

A hypothesis proposes a relationship between two or more variables. For example: *Political participation* INCREASES with *education.* This simple assertion can be seen as a hypothesis. It has a subject (the variable, *political participation*), a connective verb (a relationship, INCREASES), and an object (the variable, *education*).

To illustrate the point further:

Alienation INCREASES with *poverty.*
Union members are MORE LIKELY than nonunion members to *vote Democratic.*

Or, less obviously (and, for exercise, you can identify the variables and relations):

Absence makes the heart grow fonder.
An apple a day keeps the doctor away.
Early to bed, early to rise makes men healthy, wealthy, and wise.

31

It is crucial to realize that a hypothesis is a *supposition*, as the *Oxford English Dictionary* points out, "which serves as a starting point for further investigation by which it may be proved or disproved. . . ." A hypothesis stands near the beginning, not the end, of a study, although good studies may suggest new paths of fruitful inquiry and new hypotheses.

So far, most of our examples of hypotheses have been quite simple. But to go from the straightforward to the bizarre, let me cite an experience in teaching scientific thinking. A student came to me with the following proposal for research.

> The fragile psycho-pathological type of double helical existence issuing from the precarious relationship of the colonizer and the colonized (which figuratively is similar to the relationship of Siamese twins) and their respective interaction within the colonial situation is psychologically effective, which ramifications lead to psychological maladjustments, i.e., neuroses which subsequently define the nature of the political particulars therein.

That was just the beginning of the proposal! In all that confusing language, there are lots of variables and many relationships. Sorting it out, however, yields two hypotheses. We cut it down to:

> *Colonialism* IS ASSOCIATED WITH *neurotic behavior by colonizer and colonial.*

This neurotic behavior INFLUENCES *the political structure of colonialism.*

These two hypotheses, large as they are, were somewhat manageable. The concept *colonialism* describes a well-established political situation. The relationship IS ASSOCIATED WITH was a retreat from saying CAUSES—a precaution taken in view of the limited research resources available to the student. *Neurotic behavior* is a tricky concept, but it has parentage in the literature of psychoanalytic theory; there are behaviors that can respectably be labeled neurotic. From there it becomes a matter of showing the links between the kinds of neurotic, self-destructive behavior that occur in colonial situations and the repressive and authoritarian patterns of colonial politics.

Had the student accomplished all that these hypotheses imply by way of evidence gathering, measurement, and evaluation, he would have been in line for a Ph.D. As long as he and I knew that he was just scratching the surface, his paper (bravely entitled "Colonialism: A Game for Neurotics") was good enough for undergraduate requirements.

One of the things this example illustrates is that there is often a prior step to hypothesis formation. The step is called *problem reformulation.* In the preceding example, we began with a generalized concern about colonialism and neurosis. The student elaborated that concern into a complex description of the problem. We narrowed it down by specifying variables and relationships into something that could be dealt with, at least in a general way.

33

One of the arts of social science is skillful problem reformulation. Reformulation requires, in addition to some analytic common sense, the ability to see the variables in a situation and the possible relationships between them. A good first step is to break the problem into its component variables and relationships. Writing down lists of the hypotheses associated with a problem enables you to select the ones that answer two questions: Which hypotheses are crucial to the solution of the whole problem? For which hypotheses is there information within the range of your resources? Sometimes these questions force some unpleasant choices, but they help prevent arriving at the end of a research effort with nothing substantial on which to hang a conclusion. The preceding example on "Colonialism and Neurosis" illustrates the point.

The importance of establishing a hypothesis correctly before starting off on a research task can hardly be over-estimated. The following rules will help. The *variables* must be clearly specified and measurable by some technique you know how to use. The *relationship* between the variables must be stated precisely, demonstrable, and, if possible, measurable. If these rules are not followed, the hypothesis may be unwieldy, ridiculous, or just too hard to research in view of available resources. Precise definitions and thoughtful specification of measurements are, in short, the keys.

The struggle to form a hypothesis carefully may not be enjoyable, but the questions raised in the process have to be answered sooner or later.

The hypothesis, then, provides the structure for your entire research effort, whether it involves interviews and surveys, the analysis of previously collected data, library research, or all three. The variables you have selected can be researched through library card catalogues, book indexes, periodical guides, and computer data-base searches. The relationships proposed between the variables suggest the measurement tools and standards for evaluation that you will need to use. The results of the hypothesis test are the substance of your conclusions.

Once relationships between variables have been established through hypothesis formation and testing, these relationships can be expressed as *generalizations*. Generalizations based on tested relationships are the object of science. A generalization is a hypothesis affirmed by testing. As generalizations in a field of study accumulate, they form the raw stuff of theories. But this gets us ahead of the story. For now, we need to see how the scientific method sets the procedure for research into a logical sequence.

The Scientific Method

The technique known as the scientific method is quite commonsensical. The model inquiry proceeds by steps that include:

1. The identification of the *variables* to be studied
2. A *hypothesis* about the relation of one variable to another or to a situation
3. A *reality test* where the hypothetical relationship is measured against a result

4. An *evaluation* in which the measured relationship is compared with the original hypothesis, and *generalizations* are developed
5. *Suggestions* about the theoretical significance of the findings, factors involved in the test that may have distorted the results, and other hypotheses that the inquiry brings to mind

While we have sketched here the bare bones of the scientific method, the actual procedure of research does not always start directly with hypothesis formation. As a preliminary to stating hypotheses, social scientists will often examine the data collected in a subject area to see if there are connections between the variables. The relationships brought to light by various statistical processes frequently suggest the hypotheses it would be fruitful to explore. Occasionally, simply getting involved with a set of data triggers an interesting thought, a chance insight, or a new idea. A great quantity of data has been generated over the past few decades, so researchers can usually avoid having to begin at the beginning with every inquiry. The analysis of existing data can be extremely helpful in isolating new data needed to test a crucial relationship.

This is only an outline of the scientific method. In the hands of a skilled analyst, other elements are introduced, such as the use of alternative forms of measuring results, detailed conceptual analysis of the variable description, relationships between one's own study and others, tests of the validity of the measuring instruments, the use of experimental and control groups, and, equally important, careful conjecture that goes beyond what is established in the test itself. These embellishments on the methodology, however, relate more to the tools used in carrying on the method than to the method itself.

The point is that *the scientific method seeks to test thoughts against reality in a disciplined manner, with each step in the process made explicit.*

Consider the differences between two kinds of studies: (1) An empirical scientific study in which the author states his or her values, forms hypotheses, lays out a testing procedure, carefully selects and discusses measurements, produces a specific result, and relates this to the hypotheses. (2) A nonscientific study in which the author expresses values, develops a general thesis, examines relevant examples, and states the conclusions.

Notice that the tension between thought and investigation is present in both studies. But one important difference is the feasibility of checking the validity of the conclusions in the first example as opposed to the second, by repeating the study. "Replication" is the word social scientists use to indicate the ability to repeat a study as a way of checking on its validity. Replication constitutes a very strong test of a good study because it can reveal the errors that might have crept in through the procedures and evaluative judgments contained in the principal study.

A second difficulty with a nonscientific study lies in the problem of relating one study to another. Have you ever been annoyed in a discussion when someone asks you to "define your terms"? Have you ever gotten into arguments that end with, "How can you tell that is true?" A good scientific study presents all the information needed to see what took place. If standard variable definitions are used, a study of alienation and its relation to work, for example, can easily be added to a study of alienation and its relation to alcoholism, or crime, or whatever. Different studies of the same variables using different measures can be compared to see if measurement techniques create alternative results. The point, once again, is that science regulates and specifies the relationship between thought and investigation in such a way that others may know what exactly has been done.

The Many Roles of Theory

Science rests its claim to authority upon its firm basis in something called "reality." We have occasionally described science as, simply, reality testing. Since everybody thinks he knows what reality is, science acquires a fundamental appeal. Yet the necessary partner of realism in science is that wholly imaginary phenomenon *theory*. Without the many roles that theory plays, there would be no science (and, some would argue, there would be no understandable "reality" either).

Just as language arises out of the experience of coming to grips with human needs, so also does theory arise from tasks that people face. The hardest task is to explain what's really going on out there. Volumes have been written about what theory is and isn't. For our purposes, a theory is a set of related propositions that suggest why events occur in the manner that they do.

The propositions that make up theories are of the same form as hypotheses: they consist of concepts and the linkages or relationships between them.

Theory abounds in the most ordinary transactions

of life. There are theories of everything from the payoff of pinball machines to the inner meaning of *Peanuts* cartoons. The grandest theories of all are religious and philosophical, embracing huge orders of questions about the origin of the physical universe, the history of the species, the purposes of life, and the norms of behavior that lead to virtue and, possibly, happiness. To the faithful, such theories are made true by a belief in supernatural phenomena. These kinds of theories are presented as if they were embedded in the larger cosmos of our existence awaiting our arrival at understanding.

Social science, by contrast, generally operates from a different perspective on theory. The most conventional posture of a social scientist is one of pragmatism: a theory is only as good as its present and potential uses in explaining observations. The point of any science is to develop a set of theories to explain the events within their range of observation.

It is tempting, but misleading, to conceive of theory as something rocklike and immobile behind the whiz and blur of daily experience. Rather, theory is a sometimes ingenious creation of human beings in their quest for understanding. People create theories in proportion to needs, and the theories they create can be either functional or dysfunctional to those needs. A theory could contain a complete system of categories and generalizations about the relationships between them —but still be useless. If, for example, one were to categorize the world in terms of tall things and short things and characterize all the relationships between them, a theory would have been born, but it would be one of dubious utility—not false, but useless.

We have been discussing what theory is and is not. The next question is: What does it do? The answer is: many things. We will list four particular uses of theory in social scientific thinking:

1. Theory provides *patterns* for the interpretation of data
2. Theory *links* one study with another
3. Theories supply frameworks within which concepts and variables acquire *special significance*
4. Theory allows us to interpret the *larger meaning* of our findings for ourselves and others

Let's see if we can illustrate these four uses of theory by looking at a single study of voting behavior.[4] In an article on ethnic voting patterns in New Haven, Connecticut, Raymond Wolfinger reported the following results of a sample survey of eligible voters (see Table 2.1).

What is the message of this data? Judging from the first column, ethnic characteristics have a lot to do with party identification in New Haven. There are wide variations in support for the Democrats on the part of Irish Catholics (64 percent), Italian Catholics (37 percent), and American Protestants (9 percent), to cite a few examples. Given the pattern of this data, if you know the ethnic background of someone from New Haven, you can make an educated guess about his or her party identification.

[4]"The Development and Persistence of Ethnic Voting," *American Political Science Review* 59, 4 (December 1965): 896–908.

If we add to this information the data from the second column, the percentage of manual workers in each ethnic group, it becomes clear that working-class membership, unlike ethnicity, seems to have very little to do with party identification. The Democrats drew their greatest strength from Irish Catholics (20 percent manual workers), Negroes (76 percent manual workers), and European Jews (15 percent manual workers). Italian Catholics, on the other hand, show low support for the Democrats, yet there is a high percentage in this group who are manual workers (61 percent). To know that a New Haven resident is a member of the working class would not help your prediction of that individual's political party.

Where does theory enter in? It seems that people

TABLE 2.1   PERCENTAGE IN WORKING CLASS OCCUPATIONS AND PERCENTAGE DEMOCRATS OF A SAMPLE OF NEW HAVEN VOTERS BY ETHNIC GROUPS, 1959

Ethnic Groups	% Democrats	% Manual Workers	(No. in Sample)
Irish Catholics	64	20	(53)
Negroes	57	76	(47)
European Jews	52	15	(74)
European Catholics	48	58	(53)
Italian Catholics	37	61	(157)
European Protestants	16	35	(56)
American Protestants	9	27	(34)

Adapted from a table in Wolfinger, p. 902. Reprinted by permission. The author notes, "The table is based on 474 persons (of an original sample of 525 voters) who could be identified by religion and by place of birth of themselves, parents, or grandparents. The percentages Democratic are those who identified themselves as Democrats in response to the question: 'Generally speaking, do you usually think of yourself as a Republican, Democrat or what?' "

like to think in terms of images, analogies, and patterns. This helps to simplify complex realities and to lighten the burden of thought. Consider the usual theory of ethnic voting. It is known as the assimilation theory and holds that, as succeeding generations of ethnics move "up" in a community, ethnic behavioral patterns weaken. The first generation of Irish, for example, may vote heavily Democratic, but later generations will vote in accord with their newfound class or occupational interests and thus become more like the rest of the population. This theory evokes a kind of "melting pot" image in our minds, an analogy or *pattern* that makes it easier for us to grasp the meaning of ethnicity for politics. Without this kind of patterning, ethnicity appears as one more variable in the great equation of voting behavior. The assimilation theory suggests a dynamic and a perspective within which we can almost visualize the effects of ethnicity. The theory, as we shall see, remains to be tested against the data.

The second use of theory is even easier to understand. Theory links one study with another and helps to move social science toward cumulative knowledge. The Wolfinger study of ethnicity and social class, for example, can be related to similar studies of such factors as kinship, race, and religion to arrive at a theory as to how social class mobility influences people's behavior.[5] Jack Rothman, after analyzing seven different

[5]See Jack Rothman, *Planning and Organizing for Social Change: Action Principles from Social Science Research* (New York: Columbia University Press), 1974, pp. 311–313.

studies related to these variables, formulates a theory of the relationship between ethnicity and social mobility in order to guide community workers in organizing people:

> Upwardly mobile persons seem to form primary group ties with persons of the same "ethclass"—persons who have similar social status and who also have a similar traditional group membership, such as ethnicity or religion. . . . This suggests to the practitioner that ethclass and more traditional primary group ties are useful bases for organizing persons.[6]

Rothman's theory of "ethclass" makes us see how various kinds of data can be placed in the context of a theory that explains something important about the social environment.

So far we have seen two uses of theory in relation to this study: the *patterns* theory provides, and the ways that theory *links* one study to another.

A third use of theory, in which theory supplies frameworks wherein concepts and variables acquire *special significance,* is illustrated by the contrast between the two theories Wolfinger discusses in explaining his results. First of all, the categories which give meaning to the data are themselves the product of theories about what variables might be significant in

[6]Rothman, p. 313.

explaining human behavior. Ethnicity is thought to be more important than, say, the length of one's ears in influencing political behavior because ethnicity ties together many other aspects of our lives. For this reason, ethnicity becomes a possible key to unlocking the mysteries of voting behavior. This may seem an obvious point, but it is too easy to forget that variables always reflect some kind of theoretical conception.

In a subtler sense, theories establish the relative significance of variables. We commented briefly on assimilation theory as an explanation for the significance of ethnicity in voting behavior. As assimilation proceeds, so the theory goes, the importance of ethnicity declines. But theories are made to be tested, and the assimilation theory doesn't hold up very well in view of the New Haven data.

For the assimilation theory to hold true in the New Haven case, it would have to be demonstrated that second- and third-generation ethnics who have moved up in the class structure were *less* likely than more recently arrived lower-class ethnics to vote according to an ethnic pattern. But the data contradict this theory. Based on some additional research, Wolfinger found that second- and third-generation middle-class ethnics display a stronger ethnic voting pattern than lower-class ethnics.

The assimilation theory gives special significance to the variable social class mobility as a counter to the influence of ethnicity—a special significance which is not warranted by this study. Wolfinger develops instead what he calls a "mobilization theory" of ethnic voting. This theory states, in part, that:

> Middle class status is a virtual prerequisite for
> candidacy for major office: an ethnic group's
> development of sufficient political skill and
> influence to secure such a nomination also
> requires the development of a middle class.
> Therefore ethnic voting will be greatest when the
> ethnic group has produced a middle class, i.e. in
> the second and third generations, not the first.[7]

In the mobilization theory, upward class mobility reinforces ethnic voting. In the assimilation theory, ethnic voting is weakened by social class mobility. The essential point is that each of these two theories attributes a different significance to social class mobility as a variable in relation to ethnic voting patterns. It becomes a matter of testing the assimilation and mobilization theories to see which holds more water. As it happens, Wolfinger speculates that the mobilization theory may explain ethnic voting patterns for the first couple of generations, with the assimilation phenomena coming into play in later generations. Ethnicity persists and even intensifies as groups move from lower-class to middle-class status and thereafter it becomes less significant—at least for political purposes.

As for the fourth use of theory, interpreting the *larger meaning* of our findings, we can see that if ethnicity overrides class in all respects, then the Marxist

[7]Wolfinger, p. 905.

position that political behavior is primarily a matter of class struggle is in difficulty. If, alternatively, we do find that socioeconomic class is a significant variable, either overtly or beneath the surface, then the Marxists may have a point. Thus, a small survey of voters in New Haven, Connecticut, may, through theoretical speculation, become useful in testing a much grander conception of politics.

In discussing theory, we have presented a general outline of its commonplace uses in social scientific research. What we cannot capture is the subtlety and creativity with which people think about what they are observing. We can only say that, on the one hand, without theory social science would be a huge pile of data, statistics, and observations with no coherence and very little meaning. On the other hand, not all social science can be tied to rigorous and specific theoretical formulations. However, it is absolutely clear that the complex social problems we face need all the well-informed study we can develop. The organization and evaluation of that knowledge in theoretical form is almost as important as gathering it in the first place. History is littered with the wreckage of poorly conceived social theories.

We now have in hand the basic tools of scientific thinking. Tools, by themselves, don't get the job done. We need a plan or, as it is described in the next chapter, a *strategy* for putting those tools to work to produce some knowledge.

THE ELEMENTS OF SCIENCE

CONCEPTS INTRODUCED

Concept
Variable
Discrete quantification
Continuous quantification
Measurement
Hypothesis

Generalization
Scientific method
Reality testing
Replication
Theory

OUTLINE

CHAPTER THREE

STRATEGIES

"At the most fundamental level, knowledge is organized experience and the search for knowledge is a search for patterns of organization. The organization is always created and not discovered."

EUGENE MEEHAN

Observant readers will notice that two words, usually thought to be integral to the scientific method, rarely appear in this book. They are "fact" and "truth." What both words have in common is an air of absolutism that misleads those who become involved in the scientific approach to learning. "Fact" means, according to its word root, "a thing done." That things do get done is not disputed, but the trouble is that "things done" are perceived not by some neutral omnipotent observer, but by people. People have limited powers of perception and structures of interest that influence how they see the world. Science is a process for controlling these perceptions by making them as explicit and open to examination as possible. But the results of scientific procedure must always be taken as just that, an *attempt* to control a process that our very humanity makes difficult, if not impossible, totally to control.

For working purposes, social scientists generally regard a fact as "a particular ordering of reality in terms of a theoretical interest."[1] Such a statement means that anything identified as a fact must be seen to have tied to it the particular interests the observer brings to the study of the phenomenon. Further than that we cannot usefully go, for a philosophical forest looms in which subtle questions are raised about whether a tree that falls unobserved has really fallen, since we can't know that it did.

The term "truth" is red meat for philosophers, and they are welcome to it. Science prefers to operate in the less lofty region of falsifiable statements that can be checked by someone else. Every good scientific proposition or generalization is stated in such a way that subsequent observations may provide either supporting evidence or evidence that raises questions about

---

[1]David Easton, *The Political System* (New York: Knopf, 1953), p. 53.

the accuracy of the proposition. By making the degree of verification a permanent consideration in science, a good many rash conclusions can be avoided.

"What, then, are we to believe in?" might be the response to this noncommittal attitude toward fact and truth. If you want something absolute to believe in, it must be found outside of science. Science is a working procedure for answering questions by the refinement of experience. Scientists may develop theories of awe-inspiring power, but the way such theories meet our very human needs for belief is a personal matter separate from the meaning of science for inquiry. To "believe in science" means no more nor less than to be committed to judgments based on reality testing rather than on some other kind of evidence or mental process.

You are now familiar with basic elements of science, such as variables, measurements, and hypotheses. In this chapter we will concentrate on how to shape ideas about the world into a form that allows for reality testing. Then the process of reality testing will be broken down into its parts. Finally, we will see what evaluative steps need to be taken for understanding the results of research. The following remarks are designed as a step-by-step guide to scientific analysis. However, it must be realized that we are trying to capture only the most significant points of scientific procedure, not the finer points or the intricacies a sophisticated researcher would want to introduce. The following chapter, entitled "Refinements," adds to each element some ideas for increasing the power of your research strategy.

Please bear in mind that all we are doing here is regulating what is natural to human thought: a tension between thought and reality testing. So this chapter is organized into three sections: thinking the problem over, reality testing, and understanding the results.

Thinking the Problem Over

The biggest challenge in doing research occurs at the very beginning. Once you have met that challenge, other steps fall into place. This is the problem of limiting the topic, or, more positively, picking an approach to the topic that will most efficiently get at the thing you want to understand. Most students have had the experience of writing a long, rambling, poorly focused paper. As the need for conclusions looms with the final pages, there occasionally arises the awful feeling that from what has been said reasonably and with evidence, little that is useful can be firmly concluded. The reason for such an inglorious end can usually be found in the beginning.

Focus

Since most of us are not trained to think in terms of formulating our ideas into hypotheses and testing them, it is best to start writing things down in the way they occur to the mind: a sequence of ideas, thoughts, and notions. Ask yourself, Why am I interested in this? What is it that I am really after? See what happens. You may start with a broad topic: "Everyone seems so unhappy; people don't like their jobs; there's a general feeling of fatalism; modern society doesn't seem to have much place for the creative person." Big subjects, but there is a theme here about the nature of modern working conditions and feelings of unhappiness.

At this stage it is a good idea to try to capture these thoughts in a paragraph or two. Get it on paper! Some general reading is a good idea. It helps to map out the areas of investigation. Too much reading may be a bad idea. Don't try to get into your actual research until you have thought through the larger frame of the problem.

Suppose you wind up with two paragraphs like this:

> Society seems to be in an uproar. People are unhappy with their lives. Families are breaking down; violence is on the increase; people seem to feel that the world is cruel and headed for destruction. Karl Marx pointed out that people's social attitudes arise from their work lives. The main feature of contemporary work is the high degree of impersonalism.
>
> If people are making a living doing jobs that are not creative, they may feel powerless to control their own existence. It's a dangerous situation because these feelings could lead to extreme political behavior, such as violence, or total submission to leaders with crazy political ideas.

These paragraphs actually contain a number of variables, a network of relationships, and a whole series of hypotheses. But at least there is some indication of the possibilities for a more focused study.

At this point two levels of study could be mounted:

descriptive and *relational.* A *descriptive* study collects information about a situation. One might describe an institution, event, or behavior, or some combination of these. Good description is the beginning of science. Leonardo da Vinci's masterful notes and drawings of human anatomy enabled generations of medical scientists to advance their understanding of the body. Some specialized descriptive studies analyze information about a single variable, for example, the breakdown of families. What does it consist of? How much of it is going on? When does it occur most frequently? These studies are valuable sources for higher forms of analysis.

Relational analysis examines connections between things. The basic form consists of probing the links between one variable and another: the relation between education and voting, for example, or between intelligence and financial success. A series of relational studies can form the base for causal analysis, that special type of relational study in which the most powerful of connections between variables is isolated.

The initial thoughts on the topic given in the paragraphs above seem to imply a whole series of relations. If you are impatient to get to the root of the situation, a relational analysis of some aspect of the general problem of social uproar might be most satisfying.

Hypothesis Formation

With the topic narrowed somewhat, hypothesis formation becomes easier. The question is twofold: What are the essential variables? What are the relations between them? One intriguing piece of the problem sketched above involves two variables: *jobs* and *feelings of fatalism.* The paragraphs that were written suggest a link between the two. What is the nature of that link? What word expresses that relationship? If we leave aside causal analysis, the suggested relationship is a simple one: Boring jobs are positively associated with feelings of fatalism. Or, more precisely: A job that is uncreative is more likely to be associated with feelings of fatalism than one that is creative.

Even with all these words, we still have only two variables and one relationship: *boring jobs* ASSOCIATED WITH *fatalism.* Most studies, of course, contain several hypotheses, possibly interconnected as elements of one larger thesis. But for purposes of illustration we will stay with something less demanding.

Operationalizing Variables

To *operationalize* a variable means to put the variable in a form that permits some kind of measurement. Translating a variable into something measurable is a tricky process. If it is done right, two conditions will be met: (1) the operational version fits the meaning of the original variable as closely as possible; (2) the measurement(s) indicated can be done accurately with available resources.

How does one operationalize a variable like *jobs?* The key is in the statement of the hypothesis. Under discussion here is a specific characteristic of jobs: the variation involves creativity—more of it versus less of it. The operationalization has to do with classifying jobs according to how creative they are. What are the

55

characteristics of an uncreative job? Little control over the work, repetitiveness, minimal skill. This sounds like assembly-line work. If assembly-line work is uncreative, what is creative? A job that involves some individual control and application of skill. Maybe an artist has a creative job, or a teacher, or someone who manipulates technological processes.

Here enters another consideration. It would be easier if the research could be confined to one location. A factory often includes a variety of jobs. Are there any creative jobs in a factory? Some persons do skilled work that requires judgment. Others maintain and repair the machinery that moves the assembly line. Least creative are the basically repetitive assembly-line jobs.

What emerges here is an operationalization of the variable *jobs* in terms of three categories: line, repair, and skilled. These categories cover some significant part of the dimension of creativity in jobs.

The next task is to operationalize feelings of fatalism. The most obvious way to get at feelings is to ask about them. You might ask a sample of workers in each category, "Do you feel fatalistic?" The term "fatalism" itself has some problems, however. It is a fancy word for the feeling that we don't have much control over what happens to us. It isn't a word that people commonly use. A way of operationalizing this variable that might get you closer to everyday concerns would be to ask some questions about general attitudes toward life that reveal fatalistic feelings.

At this point, we will begin to observe the strategy actually used in a study by Lewis Lipsitz entitled "Work Life and Political Attitudes: A Study of Manual Workers."[2] The article is reprinted as an appendix to this book and a reading of it at this point will enhance the understanding of this chapter. The Lipsitz study is an example of a well-constructed and carefully presented research project. The format he uses in discussing the theoretical context of the study, the steps taken in testing hypotheses, and the larger meaning of his results provide a model of the form appropriate to research reporting.

In operationalizing the variable *fatalism*, Lipsitz put four questions to his sample of workers:

1. Will men and nations always fight wars with one another?
2. Will there always be poverty in the world?
3. Do you think the ordinary man is helpless to change some aspect of government he doesn't like, or is there something he can do about it?
4. Some people say they can plan ahead for long-range goals and then carry out their plans. Others say, "Whatever's going to be is going to be and there's no sense planning." How do you feel about it?[3]

The handy thing about these questions is that responses can be easily divided into positive and nega-

---

[2]In *The American Political Science Review* 58 (December 1964): 951–962.

[3]Appendix A, p. 155. We do not discuss the construction of scales in this text. For a detailed treatment of scales, see Hubert Blalock and Ann Blalock, *Methodology in Social Research* (New York: McGraw-Hill, 1968), Chapter 3, "Attitude Measurement," by Harry Upshaw, pp. 60–108.

tive. Someone who answers that "war and poverty are inevitable," "people are helpless to change politics," and "there isn't any use in planning ahead" could be considered fatalistic. Three of four negative responses would be evidence of more fatalism than one of four negative responses.

What we have here is a four-item scale that gives us the possibility of scoring responses in terms of the level of fatalism. There could be a score of zero, one, two, three, or four fatalistic responses.

Both variables, *jobs* and *fatalism*, have now been operationalized. Both can be measured in terms of their internal variation. Jobs are classified by their level of creativity, and fatalism is measured by a four-item scale. With the variables operationalized, the stage is set for organizing the whole inquiry.

Reality Testing

Organizing the Bibliography

With a hypothesis in mind, it is a good idea now to do some additional reading before actually beginning research. This will help you check your formulation of hypotheses and operationalization of variables against other efforts. Articles, books, and journal reports are all valuable sources for information and background. Often a single journal article on the topic will contain footnotes and bibliography that can guide you to most of the significant literature on the subject. A more sophisticated researcher would take this step first—it can save a lot of time in the thinking-it-over stage. However, beginning students often come to problems of social analysis "fresh."

Doing Research

Not many students could mount the kind of research effort suggested here. However, for instructional purposes, it is sufficient to see how an example of social science research works so that your own project can be formulated with the clearest possible strategy.

Lipsitz secured the cooperation of managers and union leaders in an auto factory in New Jersey. The hypothesis under discussion was one of a number of propositions being tested on the general subject of work life and political attitudes.

Collecting the data involves essentially two operations. First, the jobs have to be classified in terms of the operational characteristics set up for the variable. As it happens, the distinctions of line, repair, and skilled fit nicely with the descriptions actually used in the plant.

A representative sample of workers within each job category must then be drawn, unless there are sufficient resources to do the whole work force. A description of the process involved in obtaining a representative sample can be found in Chapter Four.

Each worker must then be asked to answer the questions in the fatalism scale. They can be answered orally or in writing, and the interviewer classifies the answers as fatalistic or nonfatalistic responses to the questions. The way the questions are asked is important. If they are asked by someone identified with the management, a worker might be suspicious that he or she is being personally evaluated in some way. If the questions are asked by an interviewer who seems to encourage a certain kind of answer by his or her manner or appearance, the results would not be accurate. The interview process must be made as neutral and low profile as possible.

Tallying the results is a simple process. Record the numbers of those with zero, one, two, three, four fatalistic responses by each category of worker. In the Lipsitz study, the answers were recorded for workers in each job category (Table 3.1).[4]

TABLE 3.1

Number of Fatalistic Answers

Job	None	One	Two	Three	Four
Line	0	2	3	5	2
Repair	3	2	5	2	2
Skilled	3	6	3	3	0

The figures in the table tell how many workers gave each possible number of fatalistic answers—from none through four. Looking at the data in this bare form, it is hard to see what the relationship is between the two variables, *jobs* and *fatalism*. How can these data be summarized in a way that will permit some general conclusions? Lipsitz employed an elementary device. He calculated the average number of fatalistic responses for each category of worker.

The higher the average number of fatalistic an-

---

[4]Appendix A, p. 155.

swers, the more fatalistic the category of worker. The results are shown in Table 3.2.[5]

TABLE 3.2

Job	Average Fatalism Score
Line	2.58 $(0 \times 0)+(2 \times 1)+(3 \times 2)+(5 \times 3)+(2 \times 4) = {}^{31}/_{12} = 2.58$
Repair	1.86
Skilled	1.40

The average score permits some generalization about the hypothesis: *Boring jobs are positively associated with feelings of fatalism.* The study does demonstrate a positive association: The more boring the job, the higher the fatalism score. This may seem to have provided a happy ending to the study, but there is more to concluding a research effort than simply saying, "See, I was right (or wrong)!"

Analyzing the Results

Results need to be placed in perspective. In this study, the difference in the average fatalism score varies by 1.18 points, from 1.40 for skilled workers to 2.58 for line workers. That variation is large enough to be worth comment, but a variation of, for example, .50 would be a pretty slim number to hang a hypothesis on. Considering the largest possible variation of 4.00 (from zero for the skilled category to 4.00 for the line cate-

[5]Ibid.

61

gory), we can also see that the association is not absolute by any means. The first step in analyzing the results, then, is to see how they fit in terms of the range of possible variation.

A second step is to compare the results with other studies along the same lines. Do the results regarding fatalism fit in with other efforts to relate boring jobs to such similar attitudes as powerlessness, distrust, and feelings of personal ineffectiveness? By consulting other reality tests, you can gain perspective on the utility of the one you have constructed. At the same time, other studies can provide a general check on your findings.

Understanding the Results

Evaluating Variable Operationalization

Now that you have some research experience with the subject, rethink each step of the strategy in light of what happened. There is a big difference between thinking of a way to operationalize a variable and having it work as expected in the process of research.

Some questions for this project are:

1. Did the job categories work out, or were there jobs that were hard to define as line, repair, or skilled? Were there differences within categories such as some line jobs that were less boring than others? Did some skilled jobs resemble line jobs?

2. Are you sure workers properly identified which kind of job they held? Maybe someone thought of himself as a skilled line worker and so indicated that he held

a skilled job. (A famous example of the error involved in self-identification of operational categories can be found in polls where the respondent is asked to indicate whether he or she is lower, middle, or upper class. Because the respondent's interpretation might differ from the definitions an interviewer would want to use, the answers are often misleading.)

3. Did the interview questions seem to get at the dimension of fatalism? If you encourage open-ended responses in a questionnaire, as well as forced-choice items, it is possible to get a feel for the way the questions have been interpreted. Someone might answer, "Yes, war and poverty are inevitable and average people can't plan their lives or influence politics, but this is the greatest nation in the world, God is obviously on our side, and the future belongs to us. So there!" No fatalist, this individual.

There is also the problem of a person's state of mind in answering a question. Any number of factors can influence responses. Liquor can't be sold in many states on election day so as to avoid muddling the judgment of voters. Beyond chemical disturbance is the possibility of other intervening events—if recent rumors of a layoff threaten line workers (though not others), they may be excused for feeling particularly fatalistic at the time. A good deal of social science research ignores the time dimension. The answer, obviously, is to repeat studies in different times and places. If you ask college students to fill out questionnaires, be ready for the campus wit. The jokers, the devious, and the perverse can foul up a questionnaire in many ways.

Another possible form of interference with honest responses arises from respondents who feel there is something fishy about the project, the researcher, the questions, or the presumed confidentiality of the responses. An erstwhile sophomore coed once polled the faculty of a church college about their personal use of marijuana. She did these interviews in person and assured the faculty that each response would be "confidential"—the data summaries were to be broken down by department and rank, and the final paper would then be placed in the library. However, a junior faculty member in a small department might conceivably be wary of the promised confidentiality and be less than honest in responding to such an invitation to persecution if not prosecution.

In dealing with people, science does not substitute for savvy.

Were the Measures Any Good?

Self-criticism isn't a particularly welcome task, but in social science it serves two specific purposes. Obviously, it helps to reexamine a project after you've finished to be sure that the steps along the way are sufficiently well done to lead directly to the conclusion. Reexamination serves another function, however. In dealing with something as slippery as the measurement of social phenomena, whatever is learned in the development and use of measures needs to be shared. A measure can look very impressive at the outset of an inquiry. The experience gained in actually using it, however, may turn up some unexpected weaknesses that, if stated as part of the results, can save someone else a lot of work.

In the scale used in the example, the questions do measure a kind of fatalism. But the questions all deal with large issues framed in generalities: whether war and poverty are inevitable, the possibility of individuals influencing government, and the ability of people to plan ahead. A question might be raised about whether these are the indicators of fatalism closest to people's daily lives. Concerns about war, poverty, politics, and planning are significant, but maybe not as pressing as worries about job security, family well-being, and physical threats, not to mention the noise in the car engine, the plan for the weekend, and the overdraft notice from the bank. The questions Lipsitz used for measuring fatalism could be criticized for not being close enough to the most relevant personal issues.[6]

Does this criticism invalidate the measure? No. It simply tells us more clearly what may or may not have been measured. A little more research in the field might turn up other measurements of fatalism using scales that approach personal issues more directly. A comparison of findings would increase the usefulness of your results.

Another possible criticism involves the statistics used to summarize the measures. Remember that Lipsitz used the average of scores for each job category. It would be worth checking to see what the pattern of

---

[6]In the article, Lipsitz uses a variety of measures to get at different aspects of the political consequences of factory work.

responses is *within* each job category. Table 3.3 repeats the "raw" data given in Table 3.1.

While the average tells something about the characteristics of people in each job category, it also conceals important information. Considered in terms of individual workers, it turns out that there is quite a wide variety of responses in each category. Three skilled workers gave three fatalistic answers, which makes them more fatalistic than five of the line workers and ten of the repair workers (those who gave less than three fatalistic answers).[7] Again, this doesn't make the results meaningless, it just qualifies them. It would be wrong to say that you can predict *with certainty* that an individual line worker is more fatalistic than an individual skilled worker. The average scores suggest that the odds are slightly in favor of such a prediction being correct, but it's nothing to bet the rent on.

Assorted mystics through the ages have made

TABLE 3.3

Number of Fatalistic Answers

Job	None	One	Two	Three	Four	Average
Line	0	2	3	5	2	2.58
Repair	3	2	5	2	2	1.86
Skilled	3	6	3	3	0	1.40

[7]Lipsitz examined his results more carefully than I have reported here. He looked at which questions received the most frequent positive responses, for example, and found interesting differences among job categories in their fatalism about war as opposed to poverty and other issues. Appendix A, pp. 155–157.

much of examining the entrails of birds for portents and predictions of the future. Those skilled in statistical criticism are probably the modern heirs of this profession (particularly those who are adept at finding good news and bad news in any given statistic). That statistics do not provide, in and of themselves, precise answers to social inquiries surprises some and comforts others. It is easy to say that statistics can lie, or that they never quite get the whole message across and are therefore useless. But the question is: Statistics (or measurement) compared to what? Compared to language concepts such as "more," "less," "a whole bunch," or "a little bit," statistics can be more precise.

The wrong statistic can be used as easily as the wrong word, and science is no substitute for common sense. As you learn more about statistics, you will find that researchers typically use several statistics to summarize a situation, rather than relying on a single indicator, such as an average, in order to compensate for the faults of any particular statistic.

How Do Your Findings Fit with Theories in the Field?

While a simple experiment or inquiry may answer some puzzle that is on your mind, it may also relate in interesting ways to more general issues that are contained within theories of the subject. It is mildly interesting to know that certain kinds of jobs increase the tendency toward personal fatalism—but it is a lot more interesting if that finding can be fitted in with a whole set of ideas about the human condition as it relates to work, or to the general problem (with which we started) of the breakdown of industrialized society. These are large theoretical perspectives, but theory doesn't have to be grand to be good. There are less global theories that explain key pieces of events.

Lipsitz, in the example we cite, begins and ends his article with a wide-ranging discussion of theory and previous research on the relationship between industrialization and democracy. He cites a number of other scholars who have probed the connection between the kinds of work industrialization creates, the political attitudes associated with factory work, and the way such attitudes do or do not fit in with the requirements of democratic society.

Similarly, in the exercise of writing down a couple of paragraphs on the general topic earlier in this chapter, theory surfaced in the mention of Marx and in the generalized concern with the state of modern society. If, as the Lipsitz study suggests, jobs at the bottom of the industrial order are associated with feelings of political and personal fatalism, this says something about the viability of a political system that depends on at least minimal levels of political concern and activism. An economic system that consigns large numbers of people to boring, repetitive jobs may undermine the conditions for participation in democratic government by causing widespread apathy and alienation.

In evaluating the results of a study, refer to the general readings you have done. Also, if time allows, do some more investigation of what other people have found out about jobs, boredom, and the future of society.

A noteworthy scientist once commented that "science is observation," by which he meant to suggest that getting all wound up in the details of experimental and control groups, statistics, and the rest can obscure the purpose of scientific inquiry: using your head to understand what is going on.[8] There is no such thing as the perfect experiment that explains everything about a given phenomenon. Scientific procedure is lifeless by itself. In the hands of an imaginative researcher it becomes a very useful tool, but the mind is a far more subtle instrument than any set of procedures for investigation. Where science as method ends, scientists as *people* take over.

In relating your work to theory and in speculating about its larger consequences, you have a chance to be imaginative and creative, though not undisciplined or completely fanciful. Fourier, a French socialist, extended the observation that people work better and are happier in communes to the notion that advances in human understanding would cause world history to ascend (through hundreds of years) to a situation so utopian that every day would begin with a parade, the oceans would turn into lemonade, and we would be transported across the seas by friendly whales. That's a bit much.

[8]Robert Hodes, "Aims and Methods of Scientific Research," Occasional Paper No. 9 (New York: American Institute of Marxist Studies, 1968), pp. 11–14.

THE ELEMENTS OF SOCIAL SCIENTIFIC THINKING

CONCEPTS INTRODUCED

Fact
Truth
Falsifiable statements
Verifiable observations

Descriptive study
Relational analysis
Variable operationalization
Research bibliography

OUTLINE

CHAPTER FOUR

REFINEMENTS

"Enthusiasm and deep conviction are necessary if men are to explore all the possibilities of any new idea, and later experience can be relied on either to confirm or to moderate the initial claims—for science flourishes on a double programme of speculative liberty and unsparing criticism."

STEPHEN TOULMIN AND
JUNE GOODFIELD

Developing a sense for the methodology of social science resembles learning to play pool. The basic elements of each are simple: in pool, a table, some balls, and a stick; in social science, variables, measurements, and hypotheses. Up to now, we have been looking at

73

the simple shots: a hypothesis with two fairly obvious variables and a measurement of the relations between them. In science, as in pool, the more elaborate strategies are variations on the basic technique. A good pool player never tries a harder shot than absolutely necessary; so also with a social scientist. Likewise, professionals in both fields have had to invent techniques for minimizing error and getting around obstacles. In this chapter and the next, we will discuss the elements in a slightly different order from previous chapters—hypotheses, variables, and then measurements—and explore some refinements of each. Or, in other words, we will illustrate some bank shots in the corner pocket.

Hypotheses

Hypotheses do not spring full-blown from the intellect unencumbered by a web of thoughts and preferences. Like any other artifact of human behavior, a hypothesis is part of a mosaic of intentions, learnings, and concerns. Social scientists have debated long and hard over how to deal with this reality. Some have preferred that the researcher do everything possible to forget values and other biases in order to concentrate on "objectively" pursuing work in the name of professional social science. Others have insisted that ignoring the origins of a hypothesis is inefficient because it leads the researcher to ignore basic factors in his or her own approach to data.

There is another whole set of questions related to how hypotheses fit with such structures of thought as theories, models, or, to use a more recent word, paradigms. The formation of useful theories is, after all, the end object of the exercise. Thus the relations between theory and research require exploration.

Finally, there is the somewhat more mundane, operational matter of the kinds of relationships that can be built into hypotheses. These three topics—the roles of values, theories, and relationships in the formation of hypotheses—will be dealt with consecutively.

Values and Hypothesis Formation

The notion of values is in itself peculiar. Writers have often tried to come to grips with what a value is and how one value can be separated from another. The sticky part is that values are hard to isolate. I may believe in freedom, but not freedom to the exclusion of equality, or freedom for certain kinds of behavior, such as theft. Values occur in webs of mutually modifying conditions. The confused self we all experience often may be seen acting out different sets of values at different moments, with a larger pattern visible only over a substantial time period. Still there remains a kind of consistency to human character—enough so that we can and do make general estimates of the orientation to life that people have.

Social scientists generally have resolved the problem of the relation of values to research by recommending that one's value orientations be discussed in presenting a report of a project. Because values are so intimate a part of every step of forming a hypothesis, selecting measures, and evaluating conclusions, that is a fair request. However, the specification cannot be an afterthought. The role of values has to be squarely faced at the outset of inquiry. Unless that is done, you may not see what your values are doing to your research. For example, someone who is strongly religious might do research on dating habits involving questions that are premised on the immorality of premarital intercourse. The questions used might easily reflect such a bias and invite respondents to condemn a practice that they in fact approve.

Of Theories, Models, and Paradigms

The relationship of a hypothesis, or an inquiry, to theories and models of phenomena seems commonsensical but becomes steadily more complicated when authors try to set down the relationship in writing. We know what a theory is—a set of related propositions that attempts to explain, and sometimes to predict, a set of events. By now we also know what a hypothesis is. In a rough sense, a theory is a collection of hypotheses linked by some kind of logical framework. The term "theory" connotes a degree of uncertainty about whether the understanding it offers is valid and correct. Theories, then, are tentative formulations. That which has been demonstrated to defy falsification usually is embodied in sets of "laws" and axioms.

Two other terms enter into the discussion. Scientists use the term "model" to convey an implication of greater order and system in a theory. Economists, for instance, are heavily involved in efforts to create theoretical models of the economy in which all the major variables associated with economic performance are related mathematically. On the other hand, the term "paradigm," which comes from a Latin root meaning

"Dynamite, Mr. Gerston! You're the first person I ever heard use 'paradigm' in real life."

Drawing by Lorenz; © 1974 The New Yorker Magazine, Inc.

"pattern," refers to a larger frame of understanding, shared by a wider community of scientists, that organizes smaller-scale theories and inquiries. For generations in antiquity, astronomy was dominated by a paradigm that placed earth at the center of the universe. Early observers of the heavens tried to explain all other stellar phenomena within that context; ultimately, of course, the paradigm collapsed with the advent of a much more powerful explanation.

There are few laws and axioms in social science, some vague paradigms, a good many theories, and lately some intriguing models. For those at the outset of social scientific investigation, theory is best conceived of as a guide to inquiry—a way of organizing and economizing insight so as to avoid the trivial and isolate the significant.

Induction and Deduction   There are two general modes by which theory comes into play in social science: inductive and deductive. *Induction* refers to building theory through the accumulation and summation of a variety of inquiries. *Deduction* has to do with using the logic of a theory to generate propositions that can then be tested.

The most popular image of science has researchers collecting bits of information through a gradual process of investigation and forming them into theories. The test then becomes whether or not the theory explains what is known about a phenomenon. The danger in accepting the simple view of science as induction is that the categories used in constructing the inquiry may reflect an implicit theory. What is presented as induction turns out to be a hidden form of deduction. Scientific procedure is designed to reduce such biases by requiring that the propositions in a theory be put in falsifiable form, that is, they be subject to testing. As clear as that requirement would seem to be, social investigation is so value-laden and the tools for reality testing so limited that mistaken judgments can easily be made.

Deduction is the less applied form for relating theory to research. However, under pressure of attack from critics of the supposedly "objective" nature of social science, researchers are beginning to understand that deduction subtly enters into the formation of basic concepts commonly used in hypotheses. In American culture, the pervasive conditioning to a capitalist political-economic system has led many political scientists, sociologists, and economists to take our system as the norm of the good society and to cast all nonmarket patterns of behavior into such negative categories as deviant, counterproductive, apathetic, and so on. The connotations of these labels are, in a real sense, deduced from a larger theory that implies the naturalness or rightness of one system of political economy. Yet these labels are presented as inductively arrived at "scientific" designations.[1]

Proceeding from such culture-bound assumptions, it becomes easier to argue that an individual who acts on motives other than material self-interest is "poorly adjusted" or "irrational" or in need of treatment or confinement. In fact, what is labeled as irrational behavior may serve needs repressed in a capitalist society and therefore may help one adapt to a difficult environment as, for instance, in the behavior of the poor person who buys a fancy car. Owning a car may be the one way for the person to give the appearance of success, to regard himself or herself as someone of consequence, and to attract attention from an otherwise uncaring world. That the payments deplete the food budget may strike the middle-class observer as foolish largely be-

[1]See Murray Edelman, *Political Languages: Words that Succeed and Policies that Fail* (New York: Academic Press, 1977).

cause middle-class observers, those with jobs at any rate, do not suffer the stress of constant rejection and personal humiliation.

Since deduction is a natural pattern of thought, it needs to be harnessed to scientific exploration. Very often deductions from theory provide the basic agenda of a field of inquiry. Established theories are guides to the solution of many particular puzzles. The deductive "route" is well worth trying before starting anew in the task of explanation.

There is no need to carry this navel-gazing about induction and deduction too far. A good scientific inquiry always contains those elements that make it possible for others who have differing perspectives to judge its worth. The principal reason to keep these points in mind is to be conscious of self-delusion and of the ways others are misleading in their presentation of scientific findings.

Long before you are able to deal with the formation of theories, you will be a consumer of theory retailed by others. In utilizing research results, there is a precautionary question that needs to be asked about the theory in terms of which the results are conceived to be meaningful. It is similar to the question about the values behind an inquiry, and it consists of understanding the theoretical perspective from which an inquiry is undertaken. Never read a social science work without paying careful attention to the introduction and preface—therein usually lies the key as to what the author's commitments are.

At the same time, do not be afraid to play with theoretical explanation as a guide to your own efforts. Science is very democratic and anyone can take an investigative pot shot at a theory or try to extend it in new ways. By becoming aware of the predominant theories in a field, you can save some of your own time by borrowing their vision to see what the possible explanations of a phenomenon are.

Relationships in Hypotheses

Independent and Dependent Variables Not all variables are equal. If social science only managed to show that prejudice is associated with ignorance, youth with rebellion, and IQ with breast-feeding, social scientists wouldn't have done as much as the culture has a right to expect. Are people prejudiced because they are ignorant, or ignorant because they wear the blinders of prejudice? Which precedes the other? I almost said, which *causes* the other, but did not since demonstrating causation, as we will see shortly, requires very elaborate procedures. The notion of independence and dependence in variables is a way of sneaking up on the question of causation without trying to go the whole distance.

An *independent* variable is one that influences another variable, called the *dependent* variable. As heat increases, air can hold more water. Heat is an independent variable; the amount of water suspended in the air, a dependent variable. If the air is soggy with moisture and heat goes down, water starts falling out of the air—which even social scientists refer to as rain.

In the example presented in Chapter Three on boring jobs and feelings of fatalism, Lipsitz suggests that boring jobs are the independent variable and fatalism the dependent variable. The creative possibilities

81

of a job influence the kinds of attitudes people have about life in general. However, it might work the other way around—fatalistic attitudes could lead people to take jobs that involve little creativity.

There's nothing very tricky about the notion of independence and dependence. But there is something tricky about the fact that the relationship of independence and dependence is a figment of the researcher's imagination until demonstrated convincingly. Researchers *hypothesize* relationships of independence and dependence: they invent them, and then they try by reality testing to see if the relationships actually work out that way.

The question of independent and dependent variables can be more clearly understood when seen in the form social scientists are fondest of—tables. Tables are a method of presenting data, but behind a table is often a hypothesis that escapes the attention of the novice.

Consider Table 4.1. Which is the independent variable? Which the dependent variable? How would you reconstruct the hypothesis that this data supports?

TABLE 4.1   POLITICAL ACTIVITY AMONG BLACKS AND WHITES

	Blacks	Whites
Written or spoken to Congressman	13%	18%
Worked to elect a political candidate	12	11
Given money to a candidate or political party	11	17
Belong to a political club	10	12

NOTE: From William Brink and Louis Harris, *Black and White* (New York: Simon and Schuster, 1966). Data taken from a survey commissioned by *Newsweek* magazine in 1966, based on a national sample. N = 1,059 blacks and 1,088 whites.

82

The two variables are *race* and *political activity*. What does the data say about the relationship between these two variables? The answer is that whites are slightly more involved than blacks in some kinds of political activities. Race influences participation. Therefore, race is the presumed *independent* variable and participation is the *dependent* variable. To check on the assignment of the labels "independent" and "dependent," reverse the hypothesis: Could the level of political activity influence what race a person is? No.

Table 4.1 illustrates the form in which tables are usually presented. The independent variable is listed across the *top* and the dependent variable down the *side*. By presenting tables in this standard fashion, researchers can locate the relationship without having to think about it. Nevertheless, it is a very good practice when looking at a table to formulate the hypotheses it is supposed to test. The author may have reversed the usual location of the independent and dependent variables for reasons of emphasis, style, or convenience.

In the race–political activity illustration, the independent and dependent variables are easily identified. The relationship is nonreversible. That is not always the case. In one part of the Lipsitz study, he reports data on the mental health scores of male factory workers in their forties (Table 4.2).[2]

The relationship between the variables *job classification* and *mental health scores* in Table 4.2 could conceivably be stated either way, and Lipsitz recog-

[2]See Lipsitz, Appendix A, p. 162.

TABLE 4.2

Job	Percentage with Good Mental Health Scores	Number in Category
Skilled	56%	45
High semiskilled	41	98
Ordinary semiskilled	38	82
Repetitive semiskilled	26	73
Repetitive machine-paced only (subdivision of preceding category)	16	32

nizes this. It might be claimed that the level of occupation influences mental health. A more creative job helps the mind function better. The reverse is also possible: An individual's mental health may influence what kind of work he or she is able to get. Mentally distressed persons have a hard time getting skilled jobs. Lipsitz was interested in the first of these propositions and uses other evidence to establish that it is the more likely explanation of the two.[3] He was trying to suggest through measurements of several variables that assembly-line work may create attitudes that are not healthy in a democracy.

Notice in the example above that Lipsitz violates the rule of thumb about the placement of variables: His presumed independent variable, *job classification*, is located on the side and the dependent variable, *mental health scores*, is listed on the top of the table. The rea-

[3]Appendix A, note 20, p. 163.

son for this is simply convenience: It saves space to do it that way. This is one more reason to formulate in your mind the hypothesis that is being tested in the tabular presentation of data.

Alternative, Antecedent, and Intervening Variables   One of the central problems in developing strong hypotheses lies in understanding how variables stand in relation to each other. In hypothesizing relationships between variables, you need to be aware of variables other than the ones you have selected that may be involved in producing changes in a relationship. Social scientists commonly refer to alternative, antecedent, and intervening variables.

All three terms have commonsense meanings. An alternative variable is an additional independent variable that influences changes in the dependent variable. An antecedent is something that comes before. The antecedent of birth is conception. To intervene means to come between. Richard Nixon would have been the president of the United States on the occasion of the Bicentennial had not a custodian at the Watergate building intervened and called the police to report the break-in that ultimately led to Nixon's resignation from the presidency. We will illustrate each of these concepts more precisely.

If one considers the variables which influence whether a person votes, several appear: attitudes toward the system, the difficulty of registration procedures, the weather on election day, the person's level of information about politics, and so on. These are alternative variables. To establish the link between any one of these variables and voting participation is useful

85

nonetheless, though a complete account of why people do or do not vote would have to include the influence of all the significant alternative variables.

A classic illustration of an antecedent variable comes from the history of research on voting behavior. It became obvious early on that more highly educated people tend to vote Republican. From that relationship, it could be implied that smart people are conservative. However, it turns out that there is a powerful antecedent variable which influences both the *level of education* and *voting behavior: parental wealth*. Those who are highly educated tend to come from wealthier families, and wealthier families are more likely to vote Republican. What was being measured in the correlation of *education* with *voting behavior* was really the influence of *parental wealth* on the political preferences of their children.

As for intervening variables, suppose you are told that Hollygood Bread has fewer calories per slice than six other brands. The advertising leads you to assume that the independent variable is Hollygood's special formula for low-calorie dough. You come to find out that the real reason for the difference is that the Hollygood Company slices its bread thinner than the others. The dough actually has about as many calories as Sunshaft Bread or even Wondergoo. The thinness of the slice is the intervening variable between quality of dough and calories per slice.

To use a more elegant example, consider the relationship between education and social status. These two variables are positively associated; however, everyone knows of people who have modest educations, but have high social status. The reason is that there is another variable that enters the picture: occupational success.

To see how occupational success intervenes between education and status, think of the people you know who are poorly educated, but enjoy average status by virtue of their success at their job (group A). Now think of those who are well-educated, successful, and high in status (group B). Think of yet a third group who are well-educated, but who have had lousy luck in the job market, and have middling status by conventional standards (group C).

If you only worked with the relationship between education and status or that between occupation and status, rather than all three variables, you would miss the point of the relationship between either pair. Group A would have you thinking that there is little connection between education and status, yet group B would make it appear that status and education go together like peanut butter and jelly. Meanwhile group C, just as educated as group B, has only average status. The same confusion would result from considering only the relationship between occupational success and status.

In general, well-educated people (group B) have higher status than poorly educated folks (group A). Thus, it is demonstrable that education contributes to success. However, occupational success intervenes between education and conventional social status.

The way to avoid getting trapped by alternative, antecedent, and intervening variables is to do some thinking before formulating a hypothesis. Take the dependent variable and ask yourself what all the possible independent variables might be. If you want to explain why people are fatalistic, think of all the variables that could influence such a state of mind. There are other possibilities besides the nature of their work, such as money troubles, unrequited love, background characteristics, the weather, peer-group influences. You may decide to test the original independent variable anyway just to see how much association there is. In fact, most social phenomena—perhaps *all* social phenomena—are influenced by several variables. The point of worrying about alternative, antecedent, and intervening variables is not so much to discourage investigation of what interests you as to put it into perspective so that you do not confuse association with causation.

Once you recognize the variables that have a significant influence on a dependent variable, there are ways of separating out the influence of one variable from another. The simplest technique is to "control" for one variable by holding it constant, while two others are tested for their relationship to each other. In the example of the connections between parental wealth, education, and voting behavior, one could select a sample of respondents with various levels of education from families of different wealth characteristics. If it turns out that highly educated children of wealthy families are predominantly Republican, and that highly educated children of poorer families are predominantly Democrat, you know that education is far less powerful than family wealth in shaping voting behavior. As your methodological experience and sophistication increase, you will discover a host of techniques by which these connections can be sorted out. The first step in approaching the problem of sorting out variables is to understand the different levels of relationships that are built into hypotheses.

Levels of Relationships in Hypotheses The most distinctive characteristic of a hypothesis as opposed to most ordinary sentences is the care with which each term is specified. We have seen that selection of variables is a serious task in itself. So also with the relationships that are specified between variables. In order to stretch your imagination a little, it is worth considering systematically the possible relationships that can be expressed between two or more variables. They comprise a spectrum, and we will discuss briefly each of the relationships presented in Table 4.3.

TABLE 4.3

Relationship	Meaning
Null	No relationship is presumed to exist.
Inferential/ Correlative	A relationship is presumed, but it is a relationship that deals with degrees of influence of one variable on another.
Direct/ Inverse	A specific correlative relationship is presumed in which one variable has a predictable association with another—either one variable increases as the other increases (direct) or one increases while the other decreases (inverse).
Causal	Changes in one variable are presumed to result from variations in another.

The null hypothesis is a rather ingenious creation. Remembering always that hypotheses are imagined relationships that are then put to the test, there is something to say for positing no relationship and then testing to see if the null hypothesis can be disproved, that is, if it can be demonstrated that some relationship does indeed exist.

The utility of the null hypothesis is that the case is not prejudged—you are not caught defending a relationship specified beforehand. In addition to withholding commitment to a specific relationship, you are also leaving open the possibility that one of the more substantial relationships may characterize the connection between the variables. It may be that there is an inferential or a correlative relationship that will emerge from the reality test. There may even be a direct or an inverse relationship, but those possibilities are left to emerge from the test itself.

The null hypothesis is admirably suited to a conservative strategy of social investigation. Causation requires an enormous burden of proof and is at the opposite end of the relationship spectrum from the null hypothesis. A null hypothesis can be disproven simply by demonstrating that there is *any* sort of association between two variables.

Inferential and correlative relationships can be tested as a preliminary to moving in on causative relationships. The lesser relationships, while they are interesting in themselves, are also screening devices. If, in the example of the relation of alienation to menial work, a correlation that is statistically significant can be demonstrated, then there is some reason to press ahead with the work of separating out extraneous sources of error that may be responsible for the correlation. That done, the alternative sources of causation may be tested to see if a causal hypothesis might be justified.

Several things need to be understood about the relationship of causation. First, it is probably the end object of social science to decide what causes what. Therefore, there is tremendous interest in establishing causality. Second, it is the most difficult relationship to deal with because it demands the highest burden of proof. To prove that "A" CAUSES "B," you need to demonstrate that:

1. *A happens before B.* Obvious, isn't it?

2. *The occurrence of A is connected with the occurrence of B.* Obvious as well, but the connections of events are not always simple to discover. Some historians, for example, find a consistent link between the diets of reformers in the Middle Ages and the elaborateness of their visions. Joan of Arc, it is claimed, ate the wrong things, fouled up her digestive system, and so became a visionary and temporary heroine!

3. *A causes B; there isn't some other variable (C) that eliminates the variation in B associated with A.* This is where the going gets tough. It is always hard to eliminate all the possible influences, save one, in a situation. The time-honored technique in experimental social science is to select two groups of subjects, duplicate as closely as possible everything in the environments of the two groups, and introduce the suspected causal variable to one group (the experimental group) and not to the other (the control group).

A classic example of the problems that arise in using the experimental-control group technique is the "Hawthorne" experiments, where one group of workers, the experimental group, was placed in a more pleasing physical environment for their assembly-line work. This experimental group consistently outproduced the control group, those working in the usual factory conditions. The trouble is that the increased

91

productivity was later discovered to be mostly the effect of another variable—the special attention given the experimental group by the managers and experimenters themselves—rather than the physical surroundings. The experimenters had unknowingly introduced uncontrolled psychological factors: The two groups were differentiated by more than physical decor, thus violating the experimental-control group procedure and invalidating the results.

Most social scientists view the understanding of causation as the culmination of a long process of hypothesis formation and testing. The usual technique is to begin with a series of experiments to isolate the one variable that has the most obvious connection to the caused event. By this means, suspected sources of causation can be identified. The remaining logical steps usually demand a very high order of experimental elaboration. Consequently, beginners in the field are better off staying with relationships that can be more easily managed.

Because social science involves issues of great personal importance, it is hard to cultivate the habit of caution in hypothesis formation. Most beginners overstate their hypotheses, which leads them into measurement difficulties and the disappointments of an overworked conclusion. In trying to decide how strong a relationship to test for, give some thought to the measurements available as well as to the data resources within reach. A completely reported research experiment always contains the researcher's speculations about the larger ramifications of the results. But these are more palatable if the study itself observes sensible limits of hypothesis statement and measurement technique.

Variables

Operationalizing Variables

Early in our discussion of social scientific concepts, we saw how language begins with the problem of assigning names to different phenomena. Social scientific language consists of agreements between people that a given behavior is properly referred to by a given name. Variable operationalizing, in a way, reverses the process by which language is formed: Start with the name of the phenomenon that interests you, and work backward to find ways of trying that name to the specific behavior to which it refers. To operationalize a variable means essentially to fit the name used for a behavior to some specific way of observing and measuring that behavior.

The word "operationalization" makes the process discussed here sound special and expert, when in fact it is commonplace in everyday life. I once heard an argument in a saloon over which people are better, Kentuckians or West Virginians. The "discussion" revolved around such items as the observation that one person's cousin's uncle's father-in-law was from Kentucky and he was no damn good. However, by comparison, it seems that the other person's former boss married a woman whose nephew was from West Virginia and he was born to be hanged! After several volleys of this sort, it became clear that the variables, *Kentuckians* and *West Virginians,* had been operationalized in terms of the affinity for criminal behavior of people living in those states.

As any science develops, the number of variable names that refer to carefully specified objects, events, or behaviors increases. There are now in the social sciences whole catalogues of variables operationalized in terms of specific behaviors and possible measurements.[4]

With a little luck the variables that interest you have already been operationalized in a variety of ways. Even so, you need to know a number of techniques for operationalization in order to gain analytical flexibility and to be critical of what other people have done. In addition, you need to learn how to get around problems that arise when variables require forms of measurement that are outside your resources.

There are two ways of dealing with a variable that, for some reason, is not amenable to operationalization: *substitution* and *division.*

Suppose your hypothesis is: *The more educated people are, the more likely they are to be socialists.* Education isn't hard to operationalize: The number of

[4]See John P. Robinson, Jerrold G. Rusk, and Kendra B. Head, *Measures of Political Attitudes* (1968); John P. Robinson, Robert Athanasiou, and Kendra B. Head, *Measures of Occupational Attitudes and Occupational Characteristics* (1969); and John P. Robinson and Phillip R. Shaver, *Measures of Social Psychological Attitudes* (1969). All are published by the Institute for Social Research of the University of Michigan, Ann Arbor.

years spent in school tells you about exposure to formal education.

Whether or not people are socialists, and if so, how socialistic they are, is quite another matter. The ideology called socialism brings together a complex of theories, versions of history, plans for action, and standards of good and bad. This bundle of things becomes all the harder to understand when it is realized that scholars of the subject have trouble agreeing on just what socialism means. Added to the difficulty of isolating a standard definition of socialism is the problem of dealing with unshared interpretations of the word on the part of the researcher, presumably trained in the formal ideological concept, and the sample survey respondent, who may think socialists are people who favor fluoridated water.

So it won't do to ask people, "Are you a socialist and, if so, how much of a socialist?" The answers to that question would generate some interesting data on self-perception, but the question would be too sloppy as a means of relating the respondents' attitudes to something as elaborate as socialist philosophy. *Substituting* for the variable *socialism* might solve some of these problems. Another variable could be found that pins down the attitudes involved more directly and deals with them in concrete terms. How about: *The more educated people become, the more they favor worker participation in management.*

The advantage here is that questions can be asked on a matter most people have an opinion about, and in terms that they can relate to. It does provide information relevant to the general hypothesis by picking up on an important element of socialist ideology even though it is a substitution.

Division is another way of dealing with a difficult variable. Behavior is very seldom simple; it occurs in the context of related actions, attitudes, and dispositions. Often the variables social scientists deal with can be seen as combinations of behavioral ingredients. The variable *alienation,* for example, is now frequently divided into four specific characteristics that are tied to the way people are thought to feel when they are alienated: normless, powerless, meaningless, and helpless. Attitude scales have been developed to try to measure each of those attitude ingredients of alienation. By combining measures of all four attitudes or feelings, you will have data that could respectably be said to have something to do with alienation.

Dimensions of Variables

Variables often have different dimensions. A psychologist measuring personality might come up with a classification of introverted and extroverted personalities. He or she might also come up with a characterization of aggressivity-passivity on a scale from 1 to 10. These represent different dimensions of one variable: *personality.*

Public opinion is usually analyzed in terms of a variety of dimensions:

Direction: The *for*-ness or *against*-ness of the opinion.
Location: Where on the scale from *for* to *against* is the opinion found?
Intensity: How strongly or weakly held is the opinion?

Stability: How changeable is it?
Latency: How close to the surface of the opinion structure is it?
Salience: How important is that opinion in relation to others the person holds?[5]

All these dimensions contain different measurement possibilities, and there is a variety of techniques available to handle them. The *direction* of opinion requires only a specification that tells whether the opinion is on the "yes" side or the "no" side. *Salience,* on the other hand, allows an ordering of opinions from no salience to very great salience. *Intensity* of opinion suggests the possibility of scaling.

Before doing much work on a variable, think over which dimension you are looking at and what the other possible dimensions might be. Select those dimensions that are most promising in getting to the core of the variable. By looking at alternative dimensions, choices can be made as to which dimensions get to the crux of the variable and which dimensions can be measured by the means available to you. At the same time, under-

---

[5]Adapted from Bradlee Karan, "Public Opinion and the New Ohio Criminal Code," The College of Wooster, Symposium on Public Opinion and the New Ohio Criminal Code, July 9–30, 1973, pp. 6–8; and Vladimir Orlando Key, Jr., *Public Opinion and American Democracy* (New York: Knopf, 1961), pp. 11–18.

Key discusses variables in terms of their *properties* rather than their *dimensions.* With respect to public opinion, he uses the term "dimension" where I have used "location." In recent usage, the term "properties" has become a general name for all the characteristics of a variable: its measurements as well as its various substantive components, or dimensions, which have acquired the more specific meaning I refer to.

standing the different dimensions of a variable provides perspective in what has or has not yet been done to understand the variable.

One of the most persistent myths about science is that it can be entirely equated with measurement. As the foregoing chapter has tried to make clear, the real creativity in science goes into the operationalization of variables and the design of hypotheses. These very often require genuine creativity. While measurement occasionally approaches an art form, it is more typically a matter of technique and the systematic application of mathematical concepts. As we shall see in the next chapter, measurement has its own logic and clever devices.

CONCEPTS INTRODUCED

Axioms	Inverse relationship
Peagmatism	Casual relationship
Induction	Variable substitution
Deduction	Variable division
Independent variable	Dimensions of variables
Dependent variable	Properties of variables
Alternative variable	Values
Antecedent variable	Models
Intervening variable	Paradigms
Null hypothesis	Laws
Inferential relationship	Ordinal
Correlative relationship	Interval
Direct relationship	Ratio

OUTLINE

CHAPTER FIVE

MEASURING VARIABLES AND RELATIONSHIPS

"He that makes Coates for the Moone, had need take measure every noone."

NATHANIEL WARD

Scientists basically measure three things: *variables, the chances that data about variables are meaningful,* and *relationships between variables.* Each of these measurement tasks has distinctive approaches

101

and statistical devices. As we look at the ideas used in accomplishing these tasks, remember that measurement almost always looks more precise than it really is.

The term "measurement" will be used rather broadly in this chapter. For the first topic, the measurement of variables, we will examine the kinds of measurement suited to different types of variables. Next, we will look at techniques for describing the significance of data obtained through scientific procedures. There are techniques for making fairly precise judgments about the chances that a set of data may be simply the result of a freakish sample rather than a meaningful measurement. In this connection, we show how sample surveys are constructed and discuss some common polling errors. Finally, we present some ideas about measuring relationships *between* variables. The objective is to grasp the basic tools for reducing data about two or more related variables into a statistic that characterizes the relationship between them.

Conventionally, measurement as a term applies only to the first of these topics. The second concerns the problem of the significance of data and uses probability which isn't, in the narrowest sense, a form of measurement. The third is often seen as a question of characterizing the association between things rather than of measurement strictly speaking. Yet all three topics have to do with establishing quantities of something: variation, significance, and association. Consequently, all three topics have been fitted under the general rubric of measurement.

Measuring Variables: Levels of Measurement

Measurement is a deceptive subject. At first, it seems simple—measurement answers the question, "How much?" This appears easy enough to answer when talking about length or weight, but not so easy when considering such common fodder for social science as information levels, personal characteristics, feelings, and actions. The reason for the difficulty resides not so much in the matter of counting up units of things as in the nature of the things being counted. Different variables have different possibilities when it comes to measurement.

Two considerations determine what kind of measurement can be attempted and, therefore, what sort of hypothetical relationships can be formulated using the variable. The considerations are:

1. The *properties* of the variable
2. The level of measurement *technique* available for dealing with those properties

Consider, for example, a variable such as *marital status*. The variable refers to a classification according to a legal definition: single (with the subdivisions of unmarried, divorced, widowed), or married (with, I suppose, the subdivisions of monogamous or polygamous?). In "measuring" someone's marital status, the property of the variable dictates that you can't do more than categorize—it's not possible to say that someone is very much married or very little married. In the eyes of the law, you either are or are not in such a status.

103

Given such a *property*, the variable *marital status* doesn't call for very fancy measurement *technique*.

The variable *intelligence* poses a different possibility for measurement. The *properties* of the variable do not limit consideration to classification: The variable has properties that imply larger and smaller amounts. This is where *technique* comes in. People have puzzled for centuries over how to measure intelligence. Efforts have included tests such as the sense to come in out of the rain—in which case intelligence can be measured in two categories: those who do and those who don't have the sense to come in out of the rain. Research marches on, however, and we have the IQ test. The IQ test gives us a reading on how well people can answer certain kinds of questions that are thought to have something to do with intelligence. This advance in technique permits fairly detailed gradations between the low and high ends of a scale associated with intelligence.

Measurement comprises an area of research all by itself. Researchers keep trying to develop measurement techniques that can explore all the properties of important variables. In order to systematize our understanding of various kinds of possible measurements, scientists have come up with a classification of the levels of measurement. The four levels are:

Nominal
Ordinal
Interval
Ratio

In Figure 5.1 the characteristics of these levels are explored. The *nominal* level doesn't quite seem like

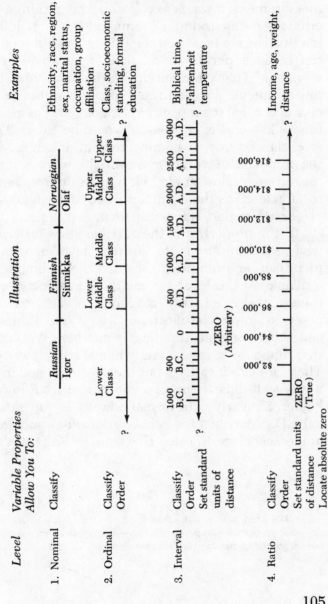

FIGURE 5.1 LEVELS OF MEASUREMENT

measurement; it refers to classifications of things. Take ethnicity for an example. If Sinnikka is a Finn and Igor is a Russian, we have said something about the properties of each person in relation to a variable called *ethnicity*. That's measurement, but not very fancy measurement. We can't rate Finns above Russians (except according to some other variable, such as fondness for vodka—and even then, it would be close). Therefore, classification, or nominal measurement, is all that the properties of *ethnicity* as a variable allow.[1] Nominal measurement, low grade as it is, pops up frequently in social science as the examples listed in the figure indicate: race, region, sex, occupation, and so on.

If the properties of the variable allow ordering as well as classification, the *ordinal* level of measurement can be attempted, provided the techniques are available. At this level, we can think in terms of a continuum, that is, an array that indicates variation, as opposed to simple classification. Class is one illustration, and socioeconomic standing is another. We can say that Alphonse is upper class, while Mack is lower class. These are classifications, but they are arranged in such a way as to link them on a continuum from lower to higher. Similarly with formal education: Angelina has a Ph.D., Mary a high school education, and Jane a grade school certificate. However, a Ph.D. isn't the

---

[1]We could, *within* each ethnic group, identify on the basis of parentage what proportion of a person's heritage belongs to an ethnic grouping, but the notion of ethnicity itself is classificatory.

same "distance" from a college degree as a high school diploma is from a grade school certificate. Ordering, yes; standard distance, no. The specification of distance or, more generally, the amount of variation between cases, is an important step up in the realm of measurement. Distance affords a decided increase in the sophistication with which a variable can be related to reality.

If standard distance can be achieved, the next level of measurement enters the picture: *interval* measurement. Here, units can be identified that indicate how far each case is from each other case. That's reasonable, but there remains one of those technicalities that causes confusion of the mind. It has to do with absolute zero on a scale of measurement.

Interval measures do not have a true zero. What is a true zero? And what good is it? In the example of biblical time, the year "zero" doesn't mean that nothing happened before then. We don't really know where true zero is in history. Zero was established in relationship to the life of Christ for religious reasons and serves as a convenient reference point for counting forward and backward. The same is true of Fahrenheit temperature. You know that 0 degrees Fahrenheit doesn't represent a true zero because -23 degrees is a lot colder than 0 degrees.

A *ratio scale* does have a true zero. A ratio scale like distance is different from an interval scale because, for example, in a ratio scale zero inches means just that —no distance at all. There can't be less than zero distance, or less than zero weight, or less than zero bananas. That tells you the formal difference between a *true* zero and an *arbitrary* zero, or one that is made up for the sake of convenience.

But, what good is a true zero? The answer has to do with what can be said in comparing observations on a ratio or an interval scale. If Hardy weighs 200 pounds and Laurel weighs 100 pounds (ratio scale), we can see that Hardy is twice as heavy as Laurel. But if the temperature is 50 degrees on Monday and 25 degrees on Wednesday (interval scale), can we really say that it was twice as hot on Monday as on Wednesday? You can try and get away with it, but you really shouldn't, because a comparison of that kind requires a *true* zero. You need to know what the total absence of heat is when making out that one day was twice as hot as another. Without a beginning point, *distances* can be established, but not *ratios.*

The reason for knowing these distinctions has to do with the kind of relationships that can be established statistically within and between variables. The job is to avoid comparison of apples and oranges. Statistics enter this text only in the form of ideas behind numbers—the arithmetic and the finer points of various statistical operations are left to more technical writings. Here we will content ourselves with a simple point (simple as statistics go). Roughly speaking:

Nominal measurement allows statistics having to do with frequency of cases in each classification.
Ordinal measurement allows statistics that describe the way the cases are ordered with respect to a variable.
Interval measurement permits comparisons of quantitative differences among cases on a scale.

Ratio measurement permits comparisons of absolute distances between cases.[2]

Because these levels of measurement are the key to how relations between variables can be approached, it is essential to figure out the appropriate level of measurement for each variable before proceeding with research. We will see the significance of levels of measurement spelled out in more detail as we turn to the problem of measuring variable relationships in the form of correlations.

Measuring the Significance and Representativeness of Data: Probability, Significance, and Problems in Polling

We now turn to three topics that fit together not so much because of their general connection with measurement, but because they all relate to understanding

---

[2]From Sidney Siegel, *Nonparametric Statistics for the Social Sciences* (New York: McGraw-Hill, 1956), p. 30. For a more recent treatment of correlation possibilities, see David Leege and Wayne Francis, *Political Research* (New York: Basic Books, 1974), pp. 287–316.

For those who are familiar with statistics, the following is a list of examples of statistics appropriate to each level:

Nominal: Mode, Frequency, Contingency coefficient

Ordinal: Median, Percentile, Spearman's *rho*, Kendall W, Goodman-Kruskal's *gamma*

Interval: Mean, Standard deviation, Pearson product-moment correlation, Multiple product-moment correlation

Ratio: Geometric mean, Coefficient of variation

the strengths and weaknesses of data that are to be analyzed.

To get hold of the statistical tools basic to scientific research, we need to become familiar with a new concept: *probability*. Probability occupies a far more important place in social science than the amount of space devoted to it in this book would suggest. Probability constitutes nothing less than a fundamental of the scientific perspective. To understand why is to come to grips with some particularly ornery habits of the human mind.

Probability refers to the likelihood or chance of something occurring. We compute probabilities about the chances of passing a course, the prospects for a date, the odds of a team winning a game. That Roget's *Thesaurus* lists so many alternatives for the word "probability"—luck, hazard, fortuity, fate, contingency, chance, and others—indicates the importance of the concept in our language.

We began by saying that science becomes useful to human beings as a way of coping with the uncertainties of life. By forcing ideas and notions out of the head and into the arena of reality and by testing them, we gain knowledge about the world. The scientific establishment is built on the power provided by the effort to escape the insecurity of uncertainty about our surroundings. However, it is characteristic of scientific knowledge that it is rarely cast in stone. Often explicitly and always implicitly, scientific generalizations are probabilistic. Science is the refinement of chance far more often than the discovery of certainty.

As an illustration of the way probability is built into social science, we shall consider two special applications of probability statistics: determining the statistical significance of an array of data, and constructing representative samples of larger populations. Yet the objective is the same in both: trying to specify the odds that a display of data reveals something more than a chance relationship between variables. If the information is based on a faulty sample or if it represents merely a freak combination of cases, then the results can't be said to tell us anything conclusive about the relationship between the variables. It is important to know that, and probability statistics provide some tools.

The first usage of probability is in establishing the likelihood of a given set of data emerging by chance. Without probing the mathematics, we can say that a distribution of data that has a chance of occurring randomly only one time in a hundred (a .01 level of significance) tells us something useful. The array of data very likely does say something meaningful about the relationship being measured, rather than simply reflecting a chance combination of responses. Some social scientists will deal only with data significant at the .01 level, while others accept .05 as the cutoff—meaning that there are five chances (as opposed to one chance) out of a hundred of the array of data occurring by chance. The significance level of data is commonly noted as part of a research report, which helps in evaluating results.

The second application of probability relates to the way samples are selected in public-opinion polling. To understand what can be done, we first need to explore briefly just what sampling amounts to. In trying to summarize the behavior of large groups of people, it is seldom possible to survey all of them. Consequently, a small group is selected that it is hoped represents the larger body faithfully. The degree of the representativeness is something that probability helps indicate. Loosely stated, the question becomes: What is the probability that a given sample reflects the larger group from which it is drawn?

There are two general techniques used in sampling: *stratification* and *randomization*. Stratification involves trying to reproduce a large population by representing important characteristics proportionately in the sample. If we tried to determine a community's attitude toward drinking by interviewing a sample of customers at a local saloon, that sample would overrepresent one segment of the public in terms of a characteristic vital to the issue under consideration. Teetotalers don't hang out in saloons. Therefore, we would have to select the sample in such a way that teetotalers have a chance of being included. If the stratification method were used to select a sample for determining voting behavior in an election, we would try to have a sample that reflected proportionately the larger population at least in terms of such significant independent variables as class, region, and education. However, the stratification (proportionate sampling of certain characteristics of voters) must be limited to a relatively small number of characteristics. Otherwise, in order to fill out the sample with representatives of all the variables in the proper proportion, we might wind up spending valuable resources trying to find a black upper-class Jew from the South who is a Republican.

Random sampling depends on selecting at random a sufficient sample of the population such that there is a high probability of reproducing the essential characteristics of the total population. If we interview five randomly selected people out of a national population of 210 million, the chances are not so good that they are truly representative—there would be a very high margin of error. With each increase in the size of the sample, provided the people are selected randomly, the margin of error decreases.

For any size population, it is possible to determine mathematically the probability that a given sample size will generate a specifiable margin of error. The margin of error drops drastically with increasing size of sample up to a point at which further increases in sample size reduce the margin of error very little. It is this point that indicates the most economical sample size. By doubling or tripling the sample size beyond this point, or even multiplying it by 10, relatively little reduction of error can be achieved.

One major problem with random sampling is that, in order to interview all of those who are randomly selected, the interviewers have to disperse their efforts and seek out respondents in all corners of the total population. Most scientific sampling uses both stratification and randomization. For example, in a national sample, one might select representative urban areas and representative rural areas (a form of stratification) and then draw a random sample within those target areas.

For their surveys of American opinion, Gallup and Harris use a stratified random sample so as to eliminate, among other problems, the inconvenience of interviewing sheepherders in the remoter sections of Nevada. The sample size is typically about 1500 persons. At this size, the margin of error is about 3 percent at the .05 level of significance. What this means is that for 95 samples out of 100, the opinions expressed by those in the sample will reflect the whole population within a range of plus or minus 3 percent. So if 49 percent of the people plan to vote for Reagan for president, 95 samples out of 100 would show Reagan getting somewhere between 46 percent and 52 percent of the vote if the election were held on the day of the poll. Both Gallup and Harris have a very impressive record of achievement in using samples of this kind to predict presidential elections, in part because they have been lucky in not drawing a "way-out" sample, one of the five in a hundred, and in part because they do stratify their samples somewhat to avoid the weird sample that might occur if simple random sampling were used.

It should be noted that there are other sources of error that creep into survey research besides the representativeness of the sample. A researcher may have selected a highly representative sample, however his or her instruments of measurement may elicit misleading answers. Common sources of error include those presented in Table 5.1.

Beyond these obvious kinds of error, there is a whole category of errors that enters into research design; these errors arise from the difficulty of being sure you are measuring what you think you are measuring. An example would be a question developed out of an interest in understanding people's personal sympathies for the poor: Do you approve or disapprove of poor persons stealing bread when they are hungry? Someone who has enormous sympathy for the poor might say, "I disapprove," because that person, while sympathizing with the poor very strongly, also has enormous

TABLE 5.1

Error	Example
Ambiguous question:	Do you think we ought to strive for peace or for a strong defense?
Symbolically loaded questions that elicit biased answers:	Do you think unborn children have a right to life? / Do you think pregnant women should have the right to choose an abortion?
	versus
	Do you favor or oppose legal abortion?
Difficult questions beyond the information level of the respondent:	Do you approve or disapprove of the ballistic missile sections of the position taken by the United States in the disarmament negotiations with Russia?
Response alternative unsuited to the subject of the question:	Do you feel better or worse about the future?
Question that includes more than one issue:	Are you more likely to favor a candidate who supports busing and a strong defense or one who has a pleasing personality?

respect for law and order. Note that the question is not meaningless; the error comes from attributing an inappropriate meaning to the responses. The question taps another variable, *respect for law and order,* in addition to the one intended, *attitudes toward the poor.*

Added to errors arising from sloppy measurement are errors introduced by the statistical procedures used to characterize the data. Statistics always distort reality to at least a small degree—that is why statisticians prefer using several techniques for characterizing data so as to hedge against the bias of a single procedure.

Measuring Relationships Between Variables:
Association and Correlation

Association

Establishing the degree of association between
two or more variables gets at the central objective of
the scientific enterprise. Scientists spend most of their
time figuring out how one thing relates to another and
structuring these relationships into explanatory theories.

As with other forms of measurement, the question
of association comes up frequently in normal discourse,
as in: "like father, like son"; "if you've seen one, you've
seen 'em all"; "an orange a day keeps the scurvy away."
In measuring the degree of association between variables statistically, scientists are merely doing what science is famous for: being rigorous and precise about a
commonplace activity.

Association can sometimes be characterized in
relatively simple ways. The effects of one variable on
another can be described in words or by statistics. "People who use Crest have fewer cavities" is a statement
that presents a relationship between an independent
variable, *brushing with Crest,* and a dependent variable, *number of cavities.*

Descriptive statistics like the median, the average,
and the standard deviation can be employed effectively
in specifying association. In the Lipsitz study, response
scores to a questionnaire were averaged to indicate the
relationship between the kind of job held and fatalistic

attitudes.[3] Percentage differences are also handy comparative instruments. If 99 percent of those on the crew of the *Santa Maria* who ate an orange every day didn't get scurvy, and 60 percent of those who ate no oranges (or any other fruit) *did* get scurvy, we can say that the chances of getting scurvy were vastly reduced by regular orange eating.

Correlation

For certain applications, statisticians have developed a more sophisticated tool for specifying relationships between variables: correlation analysis.

Correlation is usually approached as a statistical matter; here we will concentrate on the ideas behind it. Our discussion should help you recognize a correlation statistic when you see one. To understand the arithmetic and the limiting assumptions, you may consult a statistics text.

The essential idea of correlation is to describe statistically the association between variables. Assuming all other conditions are equal, a correlation statistic summarizes the movement of two variables in relation to each other.

Correlation analysis is an advance over comparing percentage differences because it allows you to capture in a single statistic both the *direction* and the *amount* of association. *Direction* refers to whether the

[3]See Appendix A, p. 155.

association is positive—that is, when variable A changes, variable B changes in the same direction—or negative—that is, if A changes, B changes in the opposite direction. The positive/negative direction is expressed by a + or − before the correlation figure. There is a positive correlation between the quantity of helium in a balloon and the rate at which the balloon rises. There is a negative correlation between the rate of rise and the weight of the balloon.

The *amount* of correlation is expressed by the size of the number on a scale from zero to +1.00 or −1.00. The scale is illustrated in Figure 5.2. Thus the correlation statistic provides a simple index of association—dangerously simple, for the mathematics behind various correlation statistics involves assumptions that require careful thought. In addition, the variety of techniques by which measures of correlation are computed causes the results to deviate slightly from the reality of

FIGURE 5.2 THE SCALE OF CORRELATION

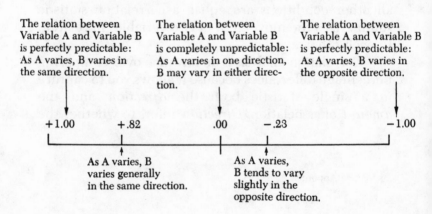

The relation between Variable A and Variable B is perfectly predictable: As A varies, B varies in the same direction.

The relation between Variable A and Variable B is completely unpredictable: As A varies in one direction, B may vary in either direction.

The relation between Variable A and Variable B is perfectly predictable: As A varies, B varies in the opposite direction.

+1.00   +.82   .00   −.23   −1.00

As A varies, B varies generally in the same direction.

As A varies, B tends to vary slightly in the opposite direction.

the data. Understanding the general techniques by which correlation operates will allow you to see some, though not all, of the problems. Nevertheless, correlation, in the imperfect world of measurement, is a valuable tool.

The techniques for computing correlation vary with the level of measurement used. If two variables are measured on a nominal scale (classification only), there is less that can be done to characterize correlation than would be the case with two variables measured on an interval scale. In fact, there are correlation techniques available for every level of measurement, and we will describe generally how they work.

Nominal-Level Correlation Nominal measurement, involving as it does simple classification, is low-grade stuff and the measure of association appropriate to it really doesn't deserve to be called correlation. The *contingency coefficient* is a statistic often used to summarize how far the actual distribution of data deviates from a distribution in which one variable is associated with no change in the other.

Suppose some researcher wishes to reverse an old proposition and test whether or not "Blondes (unlike non-blondes) prefer gentlemen (as opposed to bums)." She interviews a random sample of twenty blondes and twenty nonblondes. If it turns out that both blondes and nonblondes have similar preferences in men, then there is nothing distinctive about the preferences of blondes, and the hypothesis fails. A possible set of results illustrating the point appears in Table 5.2.

If, however, the hypothesis were correct, there would be a deviation from this kind of distribution. A statistic named the contingency coefficient computes

119

TABLE 5.2   WOMEN'S PREFERENCE IN MEN

Color of hair	Preference	
	Gentlemen	Bums
Blondes	12	8
Nonblondes	12	8

the difference between a distribution showing *no* association of the variables and one that indicates that the variables do relate in some direction. The result is expressed as a correlation.

If, in fact, the distribution came about as shown in Table 5.3, then the contingency coefficient would be −.41. The data would seem to render the hypothesis very suspect. It appears that most blondes, unlike nonblondes, prefer bums.

TABLE 5.3   WOMEN'S PREFERENCE IN MEN

Color of hair	Preference	
	Gentlemen	Bums
Blondes	5	15
Nonblondes	14	6

In more systematic language, this sort of distribution indicates some association between being blonde and preferring a certain type of man, in this case, bums. What has been measured by the statistic is the *deviation* from a distribution showing no difference in preferences. The contingency coefficient characterizes a pattern in the distribution of cases between two classifications. When the possibility exists of ordering as well as classifying the categories in the variable, establishing genuine correlation becomes possible.

Ordinal-Level Correlation Ordinal stands for order. It is this characteristic that supplies the basis for Spearman's rank correlation coefficient *(rho)* and other statistics that can be computed at the ordinal level. What can be done is to compare the ranking of cases according to their ordering on two variables. An illustration will help.

Imagine a group of 160 Jaycees singing "God Bless America." The songmaster, a systematic fellow who is secretly a Marxist, rates them according to four categories of musical ability from best to worst: Canaries, Robins, Sparrows, and Crows. He wishes to test his belief that lower-class folks are better singers than the upper crust.

So he has two ordered classifications to work with: *musical ability* ordered in terms of Canaries, Robins, Sparrows, and Crows; and *class* ordered in terms of upper, upper middle, lower middle, and lower. The hypothesis he wishes to test is whether there is any association between socioeconomic class and musical ability. The songmaster hypothesizes that lower-class people sing better than upper-class people.

If that were true, the data would have a certain pattern to it. As class went up, musical ability would go down. The lower classes would be heavily populated with Canaries, and the upper classes with Crows. Suppose he found the distribution presented in Table 5.4.

The relationship is not crystal clear from the data, but there is a pronounced tendency for lower-class Jaycees to warble more sweetly than their "betters."

TABLE 5.4   MUSICAL ABILITY BY CLASS

Ability	Upper Class	Upper-middle Class	Lower-middle Class	Lower Class
Canaries	0	0	5	30
Robins	0	10	20	10
Sparrows	5	15	15	0
Crows	35	15	0	0

We need a statistic that helps nail down the degree of association. Goodman-Kruskal's *gamma,* among other similar statistics, computes the extent to which the cases are arranged in a pattern that approximates the ordering within the variables.

Returning to the hypothesis: As we go up the class scale, does the data indicate that there is a corresponding fall off in the musical-ability scale? In the data presented in Table 5.4, the *gamma* would be $-.93$. Does this affirm the hypothesis? Yes. There is a negative correlation between class level and ability to sing.

Interval- and Ratio-Level Correlation   To do interval or ratio measurement, you need to be able to establish distances between the units of analysis. It isn't good enough to have singers arrayed in terms of Canaries, Robins, Sparrows, and Crows; the amount of distance between Canaries and Robins and the rest has to be specified. The difference in singing ability between Canaries and Robins may be quite unlike the difference between Sparrows and Crows. With the specification of distance comes the possibility of using a correlation statistic that employs the factor of distance to measure the association between variables.

Interval and ratio measurements allow the use of

a formidable-sounding statistic by the name of Pearson's product-moment correlation coefficient (Pearson's *r*).

To keep things simple, we will make up a very elementary example: the relationship in the Sheikdom of Exxit between the number of oil wells owned and the number of Cadillacs. Our "sample" consists of five oil-well owners. To see what the mathematics of the Pearson's product-moment correlation accomplishes, consider two possible arrays of data. Suppose, first of all, that there is a correlation of +1.00 between number of oil wells and number of Cadillacs. Figure 5.3 illustrates two sets of data for which that same correlation of 1.00 could be claimed.

Notice the straight solid line that can be drawn

FIGURE 5.3

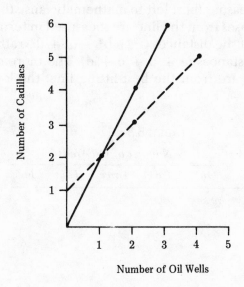

Number of Oil Wells

connecting each case expressing the following relationship between the two variables: as oil wells increase by
one, Cadillacs increase by two. A perfect correlation
also results if the straight line should happen to fall on
a different level; for example, see the broken line. It
shows that you can get a Cadillac without an oil well,
but for every extra Cadillac, it appears necessary to sink
a new well.

Now imagine an array of data in which the cases do
not present themselves on a straight line. If the data
were to appear as in Table 5.5 and Figure 5.4, no
straight line can be drawn that connects all the cases.
Pearson's *r* by a mathematical process identifies the
line that most closely expresses the linear relationship.
It is the one straight line that is closest to all the points
on the chart—the line that minimizes the distance by
which all the cases deviate from the line. For mathematical reasons (best left to mathematicians), the deviations of cases from the line are measured in terms of the
squares of the distances $(a^2 + b^2 + c^2 + d^2)$ rather than
simple distances $(a + b + c + d)$. The more distance
the cases are from the best-fitting line, the lower the

TABLE 5.5

Number of Cadillacs	Number of Oil Wells				
	One	Two	Three	Four	Five
One		1			
Two		1			
Three				1	
Four			1		
Five					1

FIGURE 5.4

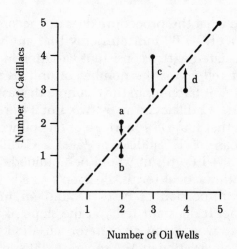

Number of Oil Wells

correlation of variable A with variable B. The Pearson's *r* for Figure 5.4 is .00.

The Pearson correlation statistic can be made to supply one other important piece of information. By squaring Pearson's *r*, we can find out what proportion of all the variation in the dependent variable is produced by the independent variable. In the case of oil wells and Cadillacs in Figure 5.4, Pearson's *r* is $+.85$, so r^2 is .72. Thus, the number of oil wells a person has explains 72 percent of the variation in the number of Cadillacs owned. Other variables explain the remaining 28 percent of the variation.

Alternatively, if all of the points fell on the line (as in Figure 5.3) and *r* is $+1.00$, then r^2 would also be 1.00 (i.e., $1 \times 1 = 1$)! The number of oil wells correlates perfectly with the number of Cadillacs, and there is no variation left over to be explained by other factors.

Notice what this procedure does *not* accomplish. A Pearson's r of $+1.00$ indicates only that any variation in A is associated with a consistent variation in B. What it does *not* tell you is the number of units B varies in relation to A. It happens in the example that as oil wells go up by one, Cadillacs go up by two. But if the situation were such that for *every* increase of one oil well, there is an increase of 1 Cadillac, or ½ of a Cadillac, or 3 Cadillacs, a $+1.00$ result would be obtained.

In mathematical terms, Pearson's r tells you only about the dispersion of cases around an imaginary straight line. It does *not* tell you the slope of the line, or, in other words, the *amount* of variation in B for every unit of variation in A. A separate statistical procedure involving advanced statistical concepts called *regression analysis* deals with this question.

Regression Analysis

The purpose of this general kind of measurement is to characterize the impact of variables on each other. Regression analysis adds a new level of sophistication to these characterizations. With regression, if you know the value of an independent variable, you can begin to predict the value of the dependent variable.

As an example, suppose you notice that your classmates differ widely in their involvement in politics: from nonvoters to political zealots. A dependent variable is born: political participation. Were you to try to explain why some people are politically active and others are not, a number of factors might be suggested (call them independent variables): personal orientation to the process of politics, parental influence, income, and prior experience with political activity. Each of these variables might turn out to be associated with the level of political participation: the question is how much variation is attributable to each independent variable. Regression analysis allows you to analyze the separate and combined effects of several independent variables.

To pursue the example, political participation, the dependent variable, could be operationalized in terms of a score derived from the number of political activities a person is involved in: voting, campaigns, contributing to candidates, engaging in protests or demonstrations, and so on. The more activities engaged in, the higher the participation score. Measurements for each of the independent variables could be similarly constructed.

As we have seen, measures of correlation make it possible to see whether income and political participation, for example, are positively or negatively related (whether participation goes up or down as income rises). Correlation also establishes how closely one varies in association with the other.

With a knowledge of the correlation of income and participation, you can estimate whether a rich person is more or less likely to be active than a poor person. If, however, you would like to have a better chance of predicting the amount of change in participation associated with each change in level of income, then regression analysis is required.

For that part of the variation in participation explained by income, it can be estimated statistically how

127

much participation varies with changes in income. Conventionally designated as *b*, this number, which can vary from zero to infinity, tells you how much change in the dependent variable occurs with each unit of change in the independent variable.

Units of income and units of participation do not compare easily, so there is a statistical technique for making them comparable for these purposes. The units can be standardized by having each unit represent one standard deviation from the average of scores for each variable. This method of standardizing is commonly done in regression analysis.[4] The resulting number is then referred to as the *Beta coefficient*, and like Pearson's *r*, it usually varies from −1.00 to +1.00. For example, if participation increases by one unit with every increase of one unit in income, the Beta coefficient is 1.00. If participation increases by one-half unit for every increase in income, the Beta coefficient is .50.

The Beta coefficient is one part of regression analysis. The other part is a multiple correlation statistic, *R* (versus Pearson's small *r* which deals with a single independent variable). *R* reports the correlation between a group of independent variables and a dependent variable. And, in parallel fashion, there is R^2 which indicates the proportion of the variation in the dependent variable explained by the group of indepen-

---

[4]There are number of technical problems in using standardized regression coefficients across samples or populations. See O. D. Duncan, *Introduction to Structural Equation Models* (Washington: Academic Press, 1975).

dent variables under consideration. Table 5.6 should help unscramble these statistics.

Taking these two measures together as multiple regression analysis, we can say that if Beta = .5, every increase of one unit of income associates with a half-unit increase in political participation. However, if $R^2 = .56$, only about half of the variation in participation is explained by income. Were we to project from

TABLE 5.6   MEASURES OF ASSOCIATION,
             CORRELATION, AND REGRESSION

Statistic*	Meaning
r	The degree of covariance between two variables $(-1.00$ to $+1.00)$
r^2	The proportion of the variation in a dependent variable explained by changes in the independent variable
R	The degree of covariance in a dependent variable associated with changes in two or more independent variables $(-1.00$ to $+1.00)$
R^2	The proportion of the variation in a dependent variable explained by changes in two or more independent variables
b	The amount of variation in a dependent variable which occurs with each unit of variation in the independent variable (zero to infinity)
Beta	The amount of variation in a dependent variable for each unit of variation in one or more independent variables where the units of all variables are made comparable in terms of standard deviations from the mean (usually varies between -1.00 and $+1.00$)

*For purposes of this table, we are using Pearson's r as the only measure of correlation. For other measures, see footnote 2, p. 104.

income to participation, we would know roughly where a given income level would place someone on a participation scale, while recognizing that other variables would be required to predict the participation level more precisely.

As a way of summarizing what has been presented so far about measuring relationships between variables and to set the agenda for the remaining discussion, look at Table 5.7.

To take the discussion a few steps further, let's look at an example. In the study presented in Appendix B by Paul Allen Beck and M. Kent Jennings, "Pathways to Participation," some of the factors that seem to influence political participation by young adults are explored. The authors were looking for the kind of background influences we have been discussing by con-

TABLE 5.7 MEASUREMENTS OF RELATIONS
BETWEEN VARIABLES

Correlation: The degree of association or covariance between the dependent variable and the independent variable, as well as the direction of the covariation (+ or −).

Regression: The amount of change in the dependent variable associated with each unit of change in an independent variable.

Multiple regression: The amount of change in a dependent variable explicable by several variables acting together. Used in conjunction with Pearson's R^2 which reports the proportion of the variation in the dependent variable explained by the independent variables in the analysis.

Partial regression: Holds other independent variables constant while estimating the impact of a single independent variable on the dependent variable.

Path analysis: A way of doing partial regression in order to reveal both direct and indirect effects of one variable on another.

130

sidering how people are socialized to political participation. The authors constructed four models of the specific relations between these variables. We will use one of the models, which deals with parental socioeconomic standing (SES), to set the stage for a more detailed illustration drawn from the "Parental Civic Orientation Model."

Working from previous research in the field, Beck and Jennings realized that the socioeconomic standing (SES) of parents would very likely have a substantial impact on whether their children are politically active when they reach young adulthood.

Beck and Jennings developed their data from a sampling of high school students interviewed in 1965 and reinterviewed again in 1973 when they were young adults. They found that parental SES explained 23 percent of the variation in young adult political participation (operationalized as nine possible forms of political involvement, ranging from voting through active participation in community decision-making). The Beta coefficient of the regression line was .20—that is, for every unit increase (measured in standard deviations) of parental SES, there was an increase of .20 units of political participation by their young adult offspring. Thus, parental SES may be seen to have a modest influence on the level of political participation of sons and daughters. The question remains: what other explanations might there be for variations in participation?

The authors were interested in measuring an alternative factor related to young adult participation: the civic orientations of parents operationalized as a set of survey items dealing with political interest, knowledge, and understanding. The question was whether these

131

attitudes, transmitted in the home, surfaced later in the level of political participation of the children. In addition, the authors wished to see the effect of parental civic orientation on the civic attitudes of high school students (in 1965) and, later, on that same group as young adults (in 1973).

By following the path from parental civic orientation through high school or youth civic orientation to participation, it would be possible to estimate some of the indirect effects of socialization. The discussion may be found in Appendix B. The technique they used, path analysis, separates out direct and indirect effects so that influence may be traced more clearly. The results are indicated in Figure 5.5.

The regression coefficients (Beta) indicate the amount of change in the dependent variable attributable to each independent variable. For example, for every unit of change in civic orientation, there are .29

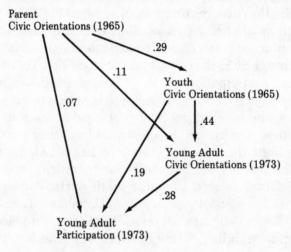

Source: Beck and Jennings (1982).

units of variation in the civic orientation of high school students.

The interesting conclusion of the study is that, although parents' civic orientation has little direct effect on participation [Beta = .07], it has an indirect effect in producing civic orientations in high school youth and young adults that may carry over into higher levels of political participation. Altogether, these independent variables explain 20 percent [R^2] of the variation in participation. This adds to our understanding of how people come to be involved in politics.

The central problem in regression has to do with sorting out the interrelated or statistically overlapping effects of several independent variables on the dependent variable. The problem can be attacked, though rarely resolved completely, by precise operationalization, by analysis of the covariance of similar independent variables, and by such advanced techniques as path analysis.

In any multivariate regression model, and especially in path analysis, there are a good many technicalities, precautions, and limiting assumptions that need to be considered before the results are taken seriously.[5] However, the logic of the analysis is what we are after here, and it is relatively straightforward. Several variables affect political participation, some directly, some indirectly. In the example, the indirect

[5]For a discussion of these problems, see Earl Babbie, *The Practice of Social Research* 2nd ed. (Belmont, California: Wadsworth, 1979), pp. 502–507. The assumptions of regression analysis make it most appropriate for ordinal, and preferably interval, level data.

effects of parental influence are more substantial than the direct effects.

As technical as the statistics make it seem, regression analysis, like science in general, begins with creativity and imagination. The first part of regression analysis is figuring out which variables to test for—and this comes from an awareness of theory and a keen sense of the subject of investigation. The usefulness of regression analysis is that it indicates the possibilities for ever more precise measurement of relations between variables in hypotheses.

Conclusion

The refinements we have discussed are themselves just the beginnings of what can be done to elaborate and improve research strategies. We have sought only to map the major pathways of understanding and technique. Further development of research skills usually comes not so much from forced marches through methodology texts as from the motivation generated by an interesting project. As the project develops, methodological matters become more significant and more rewarding to learn.

In pursuing methodological understanding, however, beware of a simple "cookbook" approach. Understand the idea of what you are doing before enlisting the specific techniques by which it can be accomplished. That, at least, is the bias of this book and the experience of this author. The wealth of detail found in the technical literature on methodology becomes much more digestible if the relatively simple ideas that underlay the calculations can be seen. Ideas provide frameworks for the mechanics of technique.

CONCEPTS INTRODUCED

Measurement technique
Nominal
Ordinal
Interval
Ratio
True zero
Arbitrary zero
Probability
Significance of data
Random sampling
Stratified sampling
Margin of error
Association
Descriptive statistics

Correlation
Direction of association
Scale of correlation
Classification
Rank order
Distance between cases
Pearson's r
Regression analysis
Slope
Beta R and R^2
Multiple regression
Partial regression
Path analysis

OUTLINE

136

CHAPTER SIX

REFLECTIONS:
BACK TO THE ROOTS

"The philosophers have only interpreted *the world in various ways; the point, however, is to change it."*

KARL MARX

Our brief study began with the very foundations of knowing: the emergence of language concepts from elementary human experience. Now the structure of method raised on this foundation can, with the aid of insights gained by our look at the operational side of science, be addressed in a more sophisticated manner. It is time to put science itself into the perspective of a broader understanding. We need to know a little more of how science fits within a larger perspective on knowledge, how scientists relate to science, and, finally, how each of us can use science as a means of increasing our ability to deal with our own environment.

Factuality, Reality, and Actuality

The scientific method often appears at first as a kind of narrow and restrictive way of reaching understanding. The demands for precision are rigorous, the statistics forbidding, and, all too often, the results difficult to read. At the same time, zealous defenders of science sometimes indiscreetly claim for science more than it can support as a strategy of knowledge. Feigning a mythical objectivity, they confuse the procedures of science for testing hypotheses with a claim to personal and professional immunity from bias and prejudice.

In trying to gain perspective on science, we can learn something from one of this century's major theorists of the human condition, Erik Erikson. In the course of his experience as a psychoanalyst, his research on various subcultures, and his extensive studies of crucial personalities in history, Erikson came to characterize understanding as multidimensional. Erikson distinguishes between three dimensions of our relationship to the world around us: *factuality, reality,* and *actu-*

ality. [1] Science, as we will see, is involved with each of these dimensions.

Of the three, *factuality* fits most closely with the popular view of scientific methodology. *Factuality is that "universe of facts, data, and techniques that can be verified with the observational methods and the work techniques of the time."* [2]

Much of what we have been considering here deals with the effort to establish that elusive item of inquiry, the fact. Earlier I hinted at a personal dislike for the word "fact." By now, however, enough has been said to make it clear that facts are not to be confused with Truth. A fact is only as good as the means of verification used to establish it and the frame of reference within which it acquires meaning. A great deal of science consists of using methodological advances to revise, modify, or even falsify "facts" and theories formerly "verified" by cruder or less sensitive techniques. By trying to verify observations systematically, we strengthen the bridge between our perceptions of the world and phenomena outside ourselves.

[1] See Erik Erikson, *Gandhi's Truth* (New York: Norton, 1969), p. 396; *Dimensions of a New Identity* (New York: Norton, 1974), pp. 33–34; and *Life History and the Historical Moment* (New York: Norton, 1975), pp. 103–104. Erikson's formulations of these concepts vary somewhat, and I have adapted them to suit the purposes of this exposition. It is interesting to note that Erikson developed these ideas in the process of analyzing how a single individual, Mohandas K. Gandhi, could penetrate the essential truths of his culture and use this understanding to change dramatically the history of India. Cf. Robert Coles, *Erik H. Erikson: The Growth of His Work* (New York: Norton, 1970), pp. 267–399.

[2] Erikson, *Dimensions of a New Identity*, p. 33, italics mine.

All the concern with thoughtful variable specification, precise measurement, and the cautious interpretation of results has to do both with developing data worthy of being called factual—and with understanding the limits of such data. While the factual view of the world seldom seems to have the glamour or subtlety of, say, the poetic view, we have tried to establish that it has a power and social utility of its own. Factuality is a necessary component of our world view, though the limitations on creating factual information, and the human characteristics we bring to the task, require a broader perspective on knowledge.

Reality, the second of the dimensions, or aspects, of understanding, is seemingly less concrete, but perhaps intuitively quite simple. Our sense of what constitutes reality is not merely a summation of factuality. *What we know as reality is, rather, a perspective on factuality integrated by the sense in which we understand these things.* Given the limitations of fact-gathering technique, the pressures of the moment, and the unconscious elements in the background of our understanding, we have to be aware that, no matter how hard we try, our understanding will never be exclusively factual. Nor need it be. Science is a discipline for finding and organizing evidence about what interests us. We then try to use that evidence to shape our view of reality. Consequently, we can legitimately ask of those who engage in science that they convey to us not just the "facts," but something of their sense of the realities reflected in their data.

A science that is to be social must engage in a kind of balancing act between the scientific principle that statements must be verified and, on the other hand, the social necessity for doing something about the crises of civilization. Verification of social theory often lags behind the necessities of social policy. In bringing together the verified and the speculative through an insightful sense of reality, we increase the possibility of an informed understanding of the world—and of our ability to change it. Developing this kind of approach to reality is no simple matter, nor can we say exactly how it comes about—except that personal commitment, experience, a willingness to suspend preconceived ideas, and good scientific procedure all play a part.

Factuality, the world of data and observation, and a sense of reality, the perspective in which we understand evidence, do not yet comprise the whole of knowledge. Erikson suggests a third dimension of existence, *actuality*, which for our purposes means *knowledge gained in and through action.*

Science creates an image of reflective inquiry, of the researcher observing phenomena to gather information and then retreating to some quiet place to assemble, digest, and characterize what can be known. Yet such a detached mode of understanding is not typical of most of us. Human beings are, it seems, more oriented to action than reflection. Actuality has something to do with how we act on (or transact between) the modes of our knowing and the occasions for behavior.

Erikson illustrates his concept of actuality by discussing his own experience as a psychoanalyst. Psychoanalysis is basically a creative form of behavioral inquiry. Erikson comments that therapy is never really a process by which a doctor prescribes some course of action to a patient, but rather a *mutual* exploration to which

141

the psychoanalyst brings training and experience, and the patient a personal history, deep feelings, and capacities for insight and action. The psychoanalytic encounter matches *potentialities* between doctor and patient.

The same can be said for social scientific inquiry. The behavior we study does not simply lie there on a slide plate or bubble in a test tube; it is formed out of the same animating principles that move the researcher as a person. The best social scientists are those who become engaged by the behavior they study. They use rigorous analysis, but they also reach into action itself as a source of understanding.

Social scientists are very circumspect about the question of personal involvement in the behavior they study. The obvious reason is that disciplined thought can be hard enough to achieve, without intruding on the feelings evoked by becoming engaged. Yet all social inquiry consists of a personal transaction with something outside ourselves. As a personal stance, detachment has its disadvantages just as involvement does. Whatever strategy is adopted, good inquiry really calls for a very high level of consciousness. The scientific method makes conscious and explicit that part of the transaction dealing with the verification of observations. There is a similar need to be highly conscious of how one's own experience and personality enter into the task of understanding.[3]

---

[3]Some classics of social science owe their particular value to the personal involvement of the authors in their subject matter; for example, Floyd Hunter, *Community Power Structure* (New York: Doubleday, 1963); Robert Lane, *Political Ideology: Why the American Common Man Believes What*

Aside from forcing a recognition of the personal elements of inquiry, Erikson suggests that experiential involvement opens up potentialities for insight. Behavior is reflexive; it emerges through transactions with an environment. Understanding the transactions experienced in an environment requires a "feel" for what is human about behavior. Such understanding demands an appreciation of factuality and a perspective on reality, but also a sense of action and what it can reveal.

Lately there has been increasing interest in what are now called "observational studies." These studies try to capture a much larger proportion of the reality that is being studied. Open-ended interviews, evocative descriptions of the surroundings, and direct reporting of personal experience characterize this approach. Behind the apparent storylike quality of observational studies is usually a thoughtful effort to test some theories and provide evidence for hypotheses. The science is not so much in variable specification and the measurement of relationships as in locating the crucial observations and drawing out their theoretical implications.[4]

He Does (New York: Free Press, 1962); C. Wright Mills, *The Power Elite* (New York: Oxford University Press, 1959); William Whyte, *Street Corner Society* (Chicago: University of Chicago Press, 1943).

[4]For some resources on these methods, see Herbert Blumer, ed., "The Methodological Position of Symbolic Interaction," in *Symbolic Interactionism: Perspective and Method* (Englewood Cliffs, N.J.: Prentice-Hall, 1969), pp. 1–60; Howard S. Becker, "Problems of Inference and Proof in Participant Observation," *American Sociological Review* 23 (1958); George McCall, "The Problem of Indicators in Participant Observation Research," in George McCall and J. L. Simmons, eds., *Issues in Participant Observa-*

Every student has gone through the process of learning something intellectually and then relearning it through experience. Science is recommended as that mode of knowing that will most benefit one's ability to establish facts, to understand the reality surrounding them, and to approach actuality with sensitivity.

Science is more an attitude and a set of general guidelines than a specific strategy. There are many possible research strategies for getting at the various levels of factuality, reality, and actuality. The choice of strategies is part of the challenge.[5]

The Morality of Science

Research on variables affecting human behavior involves us in two major kinds of moral issues. The manipulation of people in research projects can be very risky to the individuals involved. And the results of social scientific research can be used to exploit rather than to benefit people.

A famous example of the moral difficulties of manipulating experimental subjects is the Milgram ex-

tion (Reading, Mass.: Addison-Wesley, 1969), pp. 230–239; and John Lofland, _Analyzing Social Settings_ (Belmont, Calif.: Wadsworth, 1973).

[5]Some sources that will help with the problem of choosing between research strategies are: Morris Zelditch, Jr., "Some Methodological Problems in Field Studies," _American Journal of Sociology_ 67 (March 1962): 566–76; and Donald Warwick, "Survey Research and Participant Observation: A Benefit-Cost Analysis," in Donald Warwick and Samuel Asherson, eds., _Comparative Research Methods_ (New York: Prentice-Hall, 1973), pp. 189–203.

periments on obedience to authority.[6] The experiments required volunteers, under the direction of "scientific researchers," to administer electric shocks to "students" in order to encourage them to learn material that they were studying. The volunteers were told that the experiment had to do with testing a method for teaching people certain kinds of material more effectively. But the real point of the experiment was to test people's obedience to authority figures, in this case social scientific researchers. Unbeknownst to the volunteers, the electric shocks were phony, and the behavior of the volunteers themselves was the real subject of the experiment. There was a lot of deception involved here. The experiment was later explained to the volunteers and some were provided with follow-up counseling. A number of the volunteers were deeply upset to find that they had been willing to administer ostensibly dangerous electrical shocks to people in a blind response to professional authority.

Wrap the flag around an overzealous scientist and there is the possibility of a real disaster. Our own Central Intelligence Agency, in its quest for ever more powerful means of combating "enemies," used the potent hallucinogen LSD on unsuspecting subjects to see if they could then be manipulated more effectively. The experiment contributed to at least one death by suicide.

The purpose of social science should be to improve

---

[6]Stanley Milgram, *The Individual in a Social World* (Reading, Mass.: Addison-Wesley, 1977).

the quality of human life. That noble end does not justify the use of means that degrade human life, either by deceiving people into doing something they would seriously regret under normal circumstances, or by exposing their inner motivations without taking responsibility for the results to the individual.

While the ethics of dealing with experimental subjects is a matter under the control and responsibility of the researcher, a much more difficult moral problem arises when we consider the exploitative potential of social science research. The debate over the uses of social science takes place in the shadow of the controversy concerning those scientists who did the original research for atomic weapons in the 1940s. Their argument was that they were pursuing the path of science —the *uses* of science being the province of others. While social scientists have no atomic bombs to show for their efforts, the technology of social control that social science has begun to generate may well come to have a power of a magnitude worthy of the same moral concern.

We can't resolve these moral debates here, except to suggest that the cause of advancing science has no special ethical standing. To do something in the name of science doesn't excuse anybody from the moral considerations that make humane living possible.

Of Scientists, Science, and Paradigms

Science is practiced by people, not machines. Or, more accurately, science is practiced by groups of people. The major fields of social scientific inquiry are domi-

146

nated by communities of scientists, usually located at major research institutions, and tied together by a network of journals, conferences, and procedures for mutual evaluation and discussion.[7] While substantial disagreements often exist within these scholarly communities, there is usually a rough consensus about the boundaries of the principal problems, the standards for dealing with them, and the values that must inform the recommendations. No one in the American social scientific community, for example, writes about the desirability of dictatorial government. And, until recently, very few American scholars would consider seriously an openly Marxist approach to the understanding of social and political conflict.

The fact that there are communities of people involved in the enterprise of social science introduces a number of considerations that need to be reckoned with in evaluating social scientific research. First of all, few of us really like being unique or different from everyone else. Nor do people particularly enjoy having to face large problems from a point of view entirely their own. By this I mean that there is a natural psychological pressure toward conformity in all human activity, as well as in scientific inquiry.

Several factors reinforce this tendency toward conformity. One such factor is the career structure of academic disciplines. Though invisible to most students,

---

[7] An intriguing discussion of the history of science that details the role of scientific communities in structuring understanding is Thomas Kuhn's *The Structure of Scientific Revolutions*, 2nd ed. (Chicago: University of Chicago Press, 1970), on which some of these themes are based.

careers in academic institutions typically hinge on a kind of master-apprentice system. Those who study with the famous master receive the best positions and the greatest access to means of communicating their views. Ability assuredly has a great deal to do with who gets close to the master and how successfully he or she manages to develop this position into a reputable scholarly career. But the net effect of this system is a significant pressure for the perpetuation of established viewpoints, since the apprentice frequently identifies with the position of his or her master.

To this pressure for conformity, add yet another factor: the political significance of social scientific research. Researchers who probe elements of corruption in the economic system or in social welfare agencies, for example, are not likely to enjoy the favor of their targets. Even the investigation of socioeconomic power as it enters into community decision making quickly becomes controversial. Since schools and institutions are usually run by trustees who represent dominant interests, there can be career risks in certain kinds of research projects.

Another factor influencing conformity with safer forms of social explanation is that research costs money. Survey research, upon which much good social science depends, costs a lot of money and usually requires financing from governmental agencies, businesses, or foundations. The kind of professional who attracts this money is not likely to be too far out of touch with prevailing social and political ideas.

For these reasons, scientific inquiry is frequently characterized by schools of thought or paradigms that structure the way problems are defined and solved.

Yet, in the face of all these pressures, the ultimate virtue of the scientific method, as opposed to other forms of inquiry, is that the steps by which knowledge is gathered are public and open to inspection and challenge. The point of reciting the factors that prejudice inquiry is not to discredit science, since most of these factors operate in other forms of inquiry as well, but rather to emphasize yet another reason for being critical of accepted knowledge and for being scientific in your own standards of evaluation. One of the first questions to ask on reading any book, taking any course, or selecting any field of research should be: What is the dominant paradigm behind this form of inquiry? Once that paradigm is understood, you are in a position to evaluate evidence carefully.

The Radicalism of Science

After what has been said about the conformist tendencies of the scientific establishment, even allowing for the brief message of reconsideration at the end, it may seem perverse to start talking about the radicalism of science. So be it; not all has yet been said on the subject. Science can be radical in a social sense and a personal sense as well.

Scientific inquiry began as a revolt against dogma established and controlled by dominant political and religious institutions. The history of science contains some important cases of intrepid analysts who emerged from their laboratories with findings that threatened prevailing understandings in various fields of human inquiry. Some scientists have paid even with their lives for such heresies. The control of information is one of the fundamentals of political power. Scientists who insist on open and accountable procedures of information gathering and conclusion formation chip away at the power of those who would foreclose inquiry in favor of pet theories and self-serving doctrines.

More relevant to daily life are the ways in which a scientific habit of mind can contribute to your own ability to resist conditioning and to deal knowledgeably with your environment. We are all bombarded with arguments to do this or that based on somebody else's conception of what is good and bad. For most people most of the time, estimations of the credibility of sources suffice to separate the smart advice from the nonsense. But it doesn't hurt to have a means of independent evaluation.

Western culture has for a long time viewed social problems as a matter of the weakness of human nature. This approach invites introspection and the examination of personal intentions, motives, and dispositions. Social science, by and large, encourages a different approach: Look around you. Before deciding that the individual is totally responsible for his or her actions, consider the environmental factors, the structures of power, the forces of conditioning, the real dimensions of choice that face people in social situations, and the material possibilities people actually have of solving their own problems. These circumstances are sometimes more susceptible to change than are inward dispositions that grow out of a conscious and unconscious history of individual development.

Science enters into personal action as a method for disciplining the process of understanding experience.

REFLECTIONS: BACK TO THE ROOTS

The safeguards of the scientific method exist principally to control the natural tendency to project on what is observed whatever we want the world to be for our own private purposes. A discipline it is, but it becomes in practice a method of personal liberation from the narrowness of our own views, the limits of our powers of observation, and the pressures of our prejudices. Science, a discipline all may develop, can become a radical force in a world that badly needs to be changed.

CONCEPTS INTRODUCED

Factuality	Scientific community
Reality	Career structures
Actuality	Conformist social explanation
Observational studies	Scientific radicalism

APPENDIX A

WORK LIFE AND POLITICAL ATTITUDES: A STUDY OF MANUAL WORKERS*

LEWIS LIPSITZ
University of North Carolina

For centuries men have speculated about the human consequences of work. Slowly, a considerable body of information has

*I want to thank Charles Walker and Chris Argyris of Yale University,
Robert Guest of Dartmouth, Edward Gray of the United Automobile Workers, and the officers and members of UAW Local 595 for their criticism and
suggestions. A special debt is owed Robert Lane of Yale whose work helped
stimulate this study and whose disagreements with the author aided considerably in the task of clarification.

SOURCE: Reprinted by permission from the *American Political Science Review,* Vol. 58, No. 4. (December 1964), pp. 951–962.

begun to accumulate concerning the relationships between people's jobs and other aspects of their lives. Investigators have pointed out the connections between certain types of jobs and certain personality disorders, job satisfaction, productivity, attitudes toward union and management, social relations on the job, leisure activities, and other things.[1] Extending such findings, this study concludes that a particular job situation can have important effects on a man's political outlook.

Political studies have long classified individuals according to occupation, yet there have been extremely few efforts to penetrate within specific occupational categories to discover the causal triggers of occupational attitude differences. Political scientists have, on the whole, been content to work with relatively large groupings such as "semi-skilled" manual workers, "unskilled" manual workers, etc. Several efforts have been made, however, in the direction this study takes; exploring specific job characteristics and their effects on political attitudes. Seymour Lipset cites a work that established a relation between size of factory and voting Communist or Nazi in pre-Hitler Germany. William Kornhauser observes the connection between the rate of expansion of a particular industry in the

---

[1]See in particular Georges Friedmann, *Industrial Society: The Emergence of the Human Problems of Automation,* trans. Harold L. Sheppard (Glencoe, 1955), p. 276; Robert Blauner, "Work Satisfaction and Industrial Trends in Modern Society," *Labor and Trade Unionism: an Interdisciplinary Reader,* ed. Walter Galenson and Seymour Martin Lipset (New York, 1960), pp. 339–360; E. L. Trist and K. W. Bamforth, "Some Social and Psychological Consequences of the Longwall Method of Coal-getting," *Human Relations,* Vol. 4 (1951), pp. 3–38; Charles R. Walker and Robert Guest, *The Man on the Assembly Line* (Cambridge, Harvard University Press, 1952); Frank J. Jasinski, "Technological Delimitation of Reciprocal Relationships: A Study of Interaction Patterns in Industry," *Human Organization,* Vol. 15 (1956), pp. 24–28; David Armstrong, "Meaning in Work," *New Left Review,* No. 10 (July–August, 1961), pp. 16–23; and Georges Friedmann, *The Anatomy of Work—Labor, Leisure and the Implications of Automation,* trans. Wyatt Rawson (New York, 1961), p. 107.

early stages of industrialization and the political ideology of the emerging labor movement.[2] In such findings, we move somewhat closer to establishing a causal relationship between something about a particular work situation and certain attitudes or behavior of the job holders.

But more specifically, concerning the problem of job satisfaction, Lipset, writing in 1960 observed that it was yet to be shown that "job satisfaction and creativity contribute independently to political behavior over and beyond differences in status and economic conditions. . . ."[3] The present study indicates that a particular work situation, that of the automobile assembly-line, affects the political and social attitudes of the automobile workers involved. The ways in which the concrete work situation affects the worker's political attitudes are determined by the technology and social setting of the job itself. Specifically, assembly-line workers are found to be more fatalistic, more punitive, and more politically radical than other workers of comparable salary and education who work in the same plant.

I

Before proceeding to the findings themselves, it may be helpful first to consider briefly the nature of assembly-line work, in comparison with other occupational types.

The social and psychological consequences of work have been much debated. The factory is a symbol of modern life, and the assembly-line in particular has often been thought to embody in extreme form the worst tendencies of industrial work. Other analysts have argued, to the contrary, that modern industrial societies

[2]Lipset, "The Psychology of Voting," *Handbook of Social Psychology*, ed. Gardner Lindzey (Cambridge, Addison-Wesley, 1954), II, 1139; Kornhauser, *The Politics of Mass Society* (Glencoe, 1959), p. 154.

[3]*Political Man* (Garden City, N.Y., 1960), p. 237.

offer more individuals more chances for genuine work satisfaction than any previous societies.[4] It would serve little purpose here to get involved in this controversy, for even if the issues raised remain unresolved, certain facts about modern work-life relevant to our inquiry are quite clear. First, manual workers generally indicate lower work satisfaction than non-manual workers. Second, within the manual group, satisfaction varies with skill: the higher the skill, other things being equal, the greater the satisfaction. Table A.1 provides some frame of reference for dealing with the question of job satisfaction in manual and non-manual jobs.

Beyond the question of how workers respond when asked if they are satisfied with their jobs, a more important question concerns the *effects* of work; what impact the job has on a man's life

TABLE A.1 PROPORTION IN VARIOUS OCCUPATIONS WHO WOULD CHOOSE SAME KIND OF WORK IF BEGINNING CAREER AGAIN[5]

Professional Occupations	%	Working Class Occupations	%
Mathematicians	91	Skilled printers	52
Physicists	89	Paper workers	52
Biologists	89	Skilled automobile workers	41
Chemists	86	Skilled steelworkers	41
Lawyers	83	Textile workers	31
Journalists	82	Unskilled steelworkers	21
		Unskilled automobile workers	16

[4]Blauner, *loc. cit.*

[5]*Ibid.*, p. 343. The extent of satisfaction expressed is clearly in part a function of the particular question asked. For example, a group of American unskilled workers asked "Are you satisfied with your present job?" showed 72% indicating they were satisfied. Exactly what satisfaction means in such a case is not at all clear. See Alex Inkeles, "Industrial Man: The Relation of Status to Experience, Perception and Value," *American Journal of Sociology*, Vol. 66 (July, 1960), p. 6.

outside of the factory. Many writers and analysts have speculated about this. Much of the analysis of industrial work emphasizes its destructive or negative aspects and focuses attention on the elimination of skill and the increase of simple, repetitive, assembly-line style work. Yet, there have been only a few studies of assembly-line jobs.

The development of the assembly-line was part of what one observer has called the "second industrial revolution." Although overhead conveyors were employed from the 1870s on in the American packinghouse industry, they were not introduced on a large scale until 1914, when Ford's Highland Park, Michigan plant became conveyor equipped. After 1920, assembly-lines were rapidly adopted in many areas of heavy industry.

Charles Walker and Robert Guest, who made probably the most thorough study of assembly-line work, characterized the "pure" assembly-line job as involving the following six elements:[6]

1. Mechanical pacing of work
2. Repetitiveness
3. Minimum skill requirement
4. No choice in the use of tools or techniques
5. Minute subdivision of the product worked on
6. The need for constant surface attention.

The expectation that men would dislike assembly-line work is borne out by current research. Consistently, investigators have found that conveyor-paced jobs in mass production industries show lower levels of satisfaction than other manual and non-manual jobs. Blauner concludes that assembly-line work is more disliked than any other major type of work.[7] Within the automobile industry, which is the setting of this study, the position of the semi-skilled line worker is difficult. Possibilities of advancement within the ranks are

[6]Walker and Guest, *loc. cit.*, p. 19.
[7]Blauner, *loc. cit.*, pp. 346–347.

extremely slim. Wage differentials between the highest and lowest paid production jobs are small.[8]

Automobile assembly-line workers have little control over the pacing of work. The average worker on the line performs no more than five operations, remains at his station at all times, and repeats the same operations about 40 times an hour. For most workers, the work cycle is between one and two minutes, regulated by the conveyor speed.

Characteristically, the assembly-line worker is alone on his job. The technology of the line increases the worker's sense of impersonality and presents barriers to group cohesiveness. Moreover, there appears to be no adjustment to the assembly-line as time passes. The longer a man has held an assembly-line job, the more likely he is to have an unfavorable attitude toward all aspects of work experience.[9]

What do we know about the effects of assembly-line work? Compared to other groups of manual workers, assembly-line workers show few grievances, little use of pressure tactics, and much internal disunity and evidence of suppressed discontent. They permit leadership to gravitate to aggressive individuals with a strong need to dominate. They accept certain elements of their work life as inevitable, and they lack self-confidence.[10]

When Walker and Guest compared workers holding "pure" assembly-line jobs with another group of workers whose jobs were more skilled, varied and autonomous, they found that absenteeism was much higher on repetitive, conveyor-paced jobs; repetitiveness was negatively correlated with interest in work; limitations on talking were a source of frustration to line workers; mass production methods tend to increase the worker's sense of anonymity.[11] My

---

[8]Arthur N. Turner, "Impersonality and Group Membership: A Case Study of an Automobile Assembly Line" (unpublished Ph.D. dissertation, Cornell University, 1958), pp. 13–16.

[9]*Ibid.*, p. 26.

[10]Leonard Sayles, *Behavior of Industrial Work Groups: Prediction and Control* (New York, 1958).

[11]Walker and Guest, *loc. cit.*

study indicates that the differences Sayles and Walker and Guest find between different groups of semi-skilled factory workers carry over into the area of political attitudes.

II

Three samples of workers were used here as the basis for comparisons:

1. assembly-line workers, or men with jobs approximating those of the assembly-line
2. repair, relief, and utility workers
3. skilled maintenance workers.

Repair, relief and utility workers were chosen as the semi-skilled group for purposes of comparison because their jobs provided them with greater autonomy and variety than the line workers had. Repair jobs, for example, could not be time-studied and were not completely repetitive. Individual judgment and some choice of tools were required. Relief and utility workers both performed as stand-ins for men along the assembly-line, but were competent to handle many kinds of line jobs within a given department of the shop. Their work was more varied and likely to lead to a stronger sense of pride and a deeper interest in the task.

The repair, relief and utility workers, like the assembly-line operatives, would normally be classified as semi-skilled in a social class or occupational breakdown.[12] Skilled workers were also included since they would furnish an important comparison with both semi-skilled groups and might exhibit in greater detail or more extensive development tendencies found in the other groups.

[12]See, for example, the classifications employed by Albert J. Reiss, Jr., in "Change in the Occupational Structure of the United States, 1910–1950," *Cities and Society, The Revised Reader in Urban Sociology,* ed. Paul K. Hatt and Albert J. Reiss (New York, 1957), pp. 424–431.

Names were selected at random from the files of the local union. Men willing to participate were interviewed in their homes. The interview questions were almost entirely open-ended. In addition to the interviews, each man completed a questionnaire which incorporated various attitude scales and other questions. All of the men interviewed were married, native-born, and white. The three groups were closely comparable in many respects. Educationally, all three groups averaged between nine and ten years of education completed. A majority of each group was Catholic. The mean age of each sample was between 40 and 50. Assembly-line workers interviewed had been on their present jobs an average of six years; repair workers, twelve years; and skilled workers, thirteen years. Pay rates in the two semi-skilled groups varied between $2.40 and $2.74 an hour, while in the skilled group the rates ranged from $2.96 to $3.39.

The assembly plant in which these men worked was located in Linden, New Jersey. At the time of these interviews, between 2900 and 3000 men were employed at the plant. The general effort was to study intensively the political orientations of a relatively small group of men, to gain some insights of general applicability that could then be tested on a larger sample, more systematically.

III

The three work groups showed attitude differences in five areas: the job; the union; a fatalistic view of social life; the extent of preoccupations with economic problems; and the extent of sympathy and tolerance.

The Job. Assembly-line workers view their jobs with a mixture of anger and resignation. Almost all of them complain bitterly of overwork, physical strain, and monotony. They feel subjected to undue pressures because of the excessive speed of the line, but they feel powerless to control this speed. Relationships with supervisors are marked by inequality and anxiety. These men feel expendable. They know there is nothing unique about their performances at work.

All the repair, relief and utility workers have ambivalent attitudes toward their jobs. Many complain of pressure and overwork,

160

of physical and emotional strain. Yet they also note compensating factors: variety, skill, and the very important fact that the men on the assembly-line have much more unpleasant jobs than theirs.

The fifteen skilled workers present a picture of their jobs in extremely vivid contrast to those offered by the other two groups. Not a single man dislikes his job, and the degree of satisfaction is high in most cases. By and large, these men note as important the fact that they set their own pace of work; they are not closely supervised. They speak of pleasure in the creative use of their skills. They feel themselves in a position to perform useful and appreciated services for others. They have relatively good relations with supervisors. They show no sense of resignation to the inevitable; they know they can leave the corporation since they possess skills needed elsewhere. They have a certain self-confidence built on the knowledge that they have something valuable to sell.

Tables A.2 to A.6 will convey some notion of the differences in job attitudes among the three groups.

The Union. The twelve line workers show slightly favorable attitudes toward unions. Only four are altogether favorable. Five others are ambivalent, citing both good and bad features of unionism. Finally, three men are largely hostile toward unions.

Those with anything good to say about unions note "protection" as the most important union function; indeed, it is the one positive union function the line workers cite. They see the union as the only force that blunts the exploiting bent of the company. Several of the men mention seniority as an especially important kind of protection. Those who criticize the union concentrate their attention on the idea that unions are not controlled by the workers

TABLE A.2   MAJOR COMPLAINTS ABOUT JOB

| Occu-pation | Per cent citing | | | | | |
	Pressure or over-work	Physical or mental strain	No skill or mo-notony	Bad super-vision	Exploi-tation	N
Line	75	50	75	58	50	12
Repair	50	43	7	36	43	14
Skilled	13	13	0	20	7	15

TABLE A.3   MAJOR SOURCES OF JOB SATISFACTION

Occu-pation	Variety or skill	Good super-vision	Au-tonomy on Job	Better than line	Any kind of satis-faction	N
			Per cent citing			
Line	0	0	0	0	42	12
Repair	78	28	0	57	78	14
Skilled	80	67	27	67	100	15

TABLE A.4   ATTITUDE TOWARD LEAVING PRESENT JOB

Occupation	% Who would leave if possible	% Who feel stuck	N
Line	91	75	12
Repair	71	64	14
Skilled	27	13	15

but rather by a clique which serves its own interests. They assert unions are corrupt and uninterested in the rank-and-file. As a group, these men are not closely attached to their union. They give no indication of a sense of participation or solidarity.

The views of the repair, relief and utility workers resemble those of the line workers in several respects, but differ in several others. These workers show more favorable feelings toward unions generally and also toward their own union. Eight of the fourteen men have pro-union attitudes, while six are ambivalent. None is completely anti-union. Like the line workers, they stress the importance of "protection" as a union function, but four of the men also note union benefits such as vacations, company-paid insurance, etc. Within the repair group, only one man accuses unions of being oligarchical. Criticisms move in other directions and seem to be less intensely felt than among the line workers.

WORK LIFE AND POLITICAL ATTITUDES

Much as might be expected, the skilled maintenance men also show relatively favorable attitudes toward unions. Seven are wholly pro-union, while the eight others are ambivalent. This group, too, emphasizes the "protection" the union offers, but stresses union benefits even more than the other groups. None of these skilled workers show the sense of abandonment found in the line sample. And none of them criticize unions as oligarchies.

Attitudes toward Walter Reuther, President of the United Auto Workers, are quite revealing. Both the line and repair workers are sharply critical of their union head. A majority in both groups condemns Reuther as a man out for himself, personally ambitious, and uninterested in the fate of the ordinary worker. Even men who praise the UAW as a whole, and unions generally, are wholly negative where Reuther is concerned. The skilled workers, by contrast, are overwhelmingly favorable toward Reuther; praise his skill and intelligence, as well as his honesty and dedication. In all, attitudes toward Reuther are more extreme (both positive and negative) than attitudes toward unions generally, or the UAW in particular. The line workers, who are most unhappy at work, are least happy with unions and with Reuther. The skilled workers, who are most satisfied on the job, are largely pleased with unions and with Reuther. The repair group occupies a middle position in both areas.

Fatalistic Attitudes. It is sometimes argued that fatalistic attitudes do not characterize industrial man. Fatalism, it is held, is characteristic of the peasantry, lending support to rigid class distinc-

TABLE A.5   OVERALL ATTITUDE TOWARD UNIONS

	% Generally favorable	% Pro-UAW, critical of others	% Ambiv- alent	% Generally unfavorable	N
Line	33	0	42	25	12
Repair	28.5	28.5	43	0	14
Skilled	46	0	54	0	15

APPENDIX A

	% Favorable or ambivalent	% Unfavorable	N
Line	25	75	12
Repair	36	64	14
Skilled	86	14	15

tions and to the idea that the political order is not to be tampered with.[13]

No doubt citizens of industrial societies are not as fatalistic as their ancestors. Yet it is also clear that the social and technical structures of industrial societies themselves produce certain fatalistic orientations, and that these are related to the specific kinds of work men are engaged in. Those workers who are conscious of having the least control over their own lives at work show the most pronounced tendency to view the social and political worlds as unalterable.

To say the very least, it is difficult to determine the degree of fatalism comprised in an individual's outlook. In an effort to find an approximate means of measurement, individuals were scored on a fatalism scale composed of four open-ended interview questions. Table A.7 indicates the results of this scoring.

There are clear differences among the three work groups and these differences are in the expected direction. The assembly-line workers are the most strongly fatalistic. Though there is not space here to explore the types and nuances of fatalistic attitudes, a few important points need to be made. First, as a group, these men are most strongly fatalistic about the problem of war. The idea of the inevitability of aggression fits well with the picture these men have

[13]See Daniel Lerner, *The Passing of Traditional Society: Modernizing the Middle East* (Glencoe, 1958); and David Riesman, Nathan Glazer, and Reuel Denny, *The Lonely Crowd: A Study of the Changing American Character* (New Haven, Yale University Press, 1950).

TABLE A.7. FATALISM SCORES BY JOB GROUPS*

Occu-pation	Number of Fatalistic Answers					Mean score
	None	One	Two	Three	Four	
Line	0	2	3	5	2	2.58
Repair	3	2	5	2	2	1.86
Skilled	3	6	3	3	0	1.40

*The four questions that made up the scale were:
1. Will men and nations always fight wars with one another?
2. Will there always be poverty in the world?
3. Do you think the ordinary man is helpless to change some aspect of government he doesn't like, or is there something he can do about it?
4. Some people say they can plan ahead for long-range goals and then carry out their plans. Others say, "Whatever's going to be is going to be and there's no sense planning." How do you feel about it?

The four questions form a Guttmann-type scale with a reproducibility coefficient of .91, and a minimal marginal reproducibility of .671. Analysis of Variance significant at .05
t Test for Line and Repair significant at .15
t Test for Line and Skilled significant at .01

of human nature. Second, fatalistic attitudes are weakest in the area of the political potency of the ordinary citizen. These men retain the notion that a letter to one's congressman will change things. They hold to this idea despite the fact that on other questions they indicate their belief that public officials don't really care about the common person.[14]

The non-fatalistic workers in the sample stand out most strongly from their fatalistic fellows in two respects. First, they are indignant rather than merely sullen and resigned about conditions

[14]Generally speaking, these findings confirm previous ideas about working class political attitudes in the United States. For a discussion of the pessimism of working class attitudes on international affairs, see Gabriel A. Almond, *The American People and Foreign Policy* (New York, 1950), pp. 123–130.

APPENDIX A

TABLE A.8. WORK GROUP SCORES ON
LIBERALISM-CONSERVATISM SCALE[15]

	% Ultra-conservative	% Conservative	% Indeterminate	% Radical	% Ultra-radical	N
Line	0	8	33	42	17	12
Repair	8	15	54	23	0	13
Skilled	13	33	27	20	7	15

X^2—.10

they find unacceptable. Second, the non-fatalists tend to blame themselves as well as others for social failures. They emphasize the possible triumph of justice, even if only in the distant future, and the possibility of humane and rational behavior, even though many of them consider such behavior unlikely.

Economic Preoccupations and Political Radicalism. The assembly-line group is more politically radical than the other two samples of workers. This manifests itself in favorable attitudes toward governmental economic controls and antagonisms toward private ownership and the privileged orders; it is closely related to a strong tendency among the line workers to emphasize economic problems and interpretations.

The distribution of attitudes along the liberal-conservative continuum is in the expected direction (Table A.8). The assembly-line workers are the most radical, the skilled workers the least. The

[15]The Liberalism-Conservatism is taken from Richard Centers' book *The Psychology of Social Classes* (Princeton, Princeton University Press, 1949). The scale was part of the questionnaire administered with each interview. One man in the repair category never completed this questionnaire and so only 13, instead of 14, men are scored above. The Centers scale basically compares 19th century liberalism (conservative) with 20th century liberalism (radical—welfare state). The questions explore management versus labor identification; belief in the possibilities of economic opportunity; attitude toward government ownership and social insurance.

166

patterns for the three groups bear a close resemblance to the scores for skilled, semi-skilled manual workers which Centers found in a nationwide sample in the late 1940's.

Symptomatic of their economic preoccupations, two contrasts emerge among the work groups in which the line workers attach a greater emphasis to economic considerations. First, they tend more strongly to view economic problems as the most important ones confronting America today. Fifty-eight per cent of the line group ranks economic problems most important as compared with 36 per cent of the repair group and 33 per cent of the skilled workers.

The kinds of economic problems mentioned by the different groups were also quite distinct. All of the men in the assembly-line group who mentioned economic problems at all concerned themselves either with unemployment or poor working conditions; both problems very close to home. In contrast, men in the other two groups raised questions about high taxes, foreign aid, welfare excesses, salary differentials, and the demise of free enterprise.

Second, the concern with economic difficulties shows itself in responses to a question that asks about the nature of the "chains" men feel. The question was phrased, "A man once said: 'Man is born free, but everywhere he is in chains.' Does this mean anything to you?" Table A.9 arranges the response according to whether the individual saw Rousseau's "chains" in economic terms.

Table A.9 is significant not only because the line and repair workers tend to perceive "chains" in economic terms, but also be-

TABLE A.9   RESPONSES TO ROUSSEAU

	% Offering economic inter-pretation	% Offering non-economic interpre-tation	N*
Line	86	14	7
Repair	77	23	13
Skilled	27	73	11

*Percentages are based only on those who offered some interpretation and therefore exclude the "don't knows."
X^2—.02

167

cause they tend to see these "chains" as oppressive. Remisik, a repairman, typifies much of the commentary: ". . . has to earn his bread. He's chained to a job of some sort, regardless of whether it's here or any other concern. . . ." The "chains" these men see range over bills, the regimentation of factory life, and the income tax. On the other hand, most of those who offer non-economic interpretations think of "chains" without the element of oppression. Harris, a maintenance painter, serves as a good example: "Yeah, everybody is born free, true—but then we acquire chains. It has to be. There's law, regulations that we have to abide by. . . . We're always in chains, but chains can get awfully heavy in some of these countries."

Sympathy and Tolerance. None of the questions in the interview schedule was designed directly to explore dimensions of sympathy or tolerance. Yet, several of the questions seemed to elicit punitive responses from some of the men but not from others. All of these questions touched on attitudes toward "out-groups." The four questions were:

1. Why are people poor?
2. What should our policy be toward Russia?
3. Do you think it was a good idea to drop atomic bombs on Japan in World War II?
4. How do you feel about capital punishment?

Though the evidence is very skimpy and impressionistic, it appears that the assembly-line group is less sympathetic and tolerant than the others. In all of the four cases, the line workers are slightly more punitive as a group. They tend more strongly to blame the poor themselves for poverty. They were more likely to approve the bombing of Japan without showing any sympathy for the Japanese, and to recommend a policy of toughness toward Russia. Finally, they were somewhat more likely to favor the death penalty.

These findings are worth noting largely because they tend to confirm previous conclusions about authoritarianism and social class. Within this group of workers, punitive attitudes are associated with work frustration and lack of control over worklife. These facts point up the possible significance of everyday frustrations in conditioning attitudes toward outgroups.[16] The possibility that such frustrations might play an important role in shaping attitudes is one that psychoanalytic research has left open for the moment.[17]

IV

In two important areas the three groups show attitudes that are much alike but are important to describe nonetheless in order to give greater definition to the picture of working class views drawn thus far. First, a majority of the men in all three groups emphasize the manipulative nature of much of social life. They express concern about the exploiting and unfair practices of their corporation and of big business generally. Moreover, approximately half the men express concern about two-faced, deliberately deceptive tactics of the government and mass media which they see as closely related. Table A.10 shows the distribution of such attitudes in the three work groups.

Where big business is concerned, these workers see manipulative practices everywhere. A few believe big business or the rich run the United States. Others are not quite so explicit, but believe that big business is free of the restraints that bind ordinary mortals: businesses can initiate wars, bribe judges and representatives and manage to get the government to follow their dictates. In some of these men, hostile attitudes toward big business and especially to-

---

[16]Lipset points out that the unemployed, feeling resentful and alienated, are less tolerant of minority groups than are employed workers, a finding that seems related to the conclusions here about the assembly-line group. See S. M. Lipset, *Political Man: The Social Bases of Politics* (Garden City, 1960), p. 114. For a discussion of the importance of attitudes toward out-groups, see T. W. Adorno and associates, *The Authoritarian Personality* (New York, 1950), chs. 2–4.

[17]See Bjorn Christiansen, *Attitudes Towards Foreign Affairs as a Function of Personality* (Oslo, Norway, Oslo University Press, 1959), p. 59.

APPENDIX A

TABLE A.10 PER CENT PERCEIVING MANIPULATIVE PRACTICES
BY BIG BUSINESS OR CORPORATION X, AND BY GOVERNMENT OR
MASS MEDIA*

	See manip. by Corp. X or big business	See manip. by govt. or mass media	N
	(%)	(%)	
Line	92	50	12
Repair	79	43	14
Skilled	60	47	15

*The specific questions asked were:
1. How do you feel about big business?
2. How do you feel about Corporation X?
3. Do you feel there's much corruption in politics? Why?

ward their own corporation, attain a frenzied pitch and a deep
bitterness.

Most of the men feel that the corporation acts as it does because
its primary concern is profit-making. Some see businesses caught in
a competitive rat-race in which it is do or die. The methods of the
rich, as these workers describe them, are not subtle. These men
simply affirm the idea that "money talks." Very few of them have
any praise for big business. Most simply accept it as a fact of life,
unable, like the line worker Tencio, to visualize a world without it:
"Well, without big business, what could the working man do? He
gotta work for big business."

It is not particularly surprising to learn that many of these
working class men are critical of big business. But it is very much
another thing to find that almost half of the 41 men are critical of
manipulative and deceptive aspects of American government and
the mass media. The chief theme of the critics is that the government is immune to popular pressures. The general picture is of a
group of men who arrange to keep themselves in power and who
don't care about the requests of the common people. The means of
governmental manipulation are varied: nepotism, misleading prop-
aganda, suppression of information, bribery, silencing of dissent.
The credibility of the media is to some degree tied up with the

170

credibility of the government. Several of the men feel that the radio, papers, television only convey what they are told to. They are tools, willing or unwilling, of the politicians. Five men criticize the media as manipulative in their own right. All who discuss the media do so in terms of their deceptive political content.

Some of the workers who are concerned about manipulations tend in the direction of a conspiracy theory of social control. Yet few of them actually express anything resembling a theory of a hidden oligarchy or oligarchies. At most, seven men give any clear indications of holding to such a picture of American society. In all seven cases, it is the "rich," or "big business" which is said to be the ruling elite.

The remaining two-thirds of the men who criticize various manipulative practices give no indication of adhering to a power-elite theory. They criticize business, government and media for attempting to manipulate the common man, but their criticism is specific and piecemeal. They do not have any clearly formulated picture of social life, nor any precise notions about who is to blame for the seamy side of things. They are critical of the excessive power of big business and yet do not believe that big business runs the country. They can believe that people in the government attempt to mislead the public without going sour on government as a whole.

Yet, behind their vagueness and their sense of their own ignorance, most of these men actually have developed an explanation for the practices they criticize. First, they see a society directed toward profit-making. Second, they are aware of wide disparities of power. Out of these elements, these men have constructed a suspicion of human nature. It is human nature and nothing less, they say, which leads to the malpractices of business and government. Thus, it is not a particular group of evil men who are to blame, but rather the selfishness supposedly inherent in almost all of us.[18]

---

[18]Thus, most of these men are not "cabalists" as that term is used by Robert E. Lane. Describing the cabalist frame of mind Lane notes: (1) There

171

These workers generally accept the profit-motive as a satisfactory explanation of business behavior. But this does not account for governmental behavior. Why these failures, large and small, in the democratic system?

A substantial majority of the men believe that politics, like most other aspects of our society, is basically a business. Three-quarters of the line workers, 57 per cent of the repair sample, and 60 per cent of the maintenance men see politicians as predominantly self-seeking. They see elections and platforms designed to fool the public; politicians seeking to perpetuate their own domination; stealing, nepotism, the wasting of public funds, etc. A government composed of such individuals could not possibly be very attentive to the kinds of problems these workers are concerned about. It is not surprising then that they see failures in the political system. The selfish nature of politicians springs from their unfortunate and seemingly indelible humanity.

The second important area of similarity among the three groups is political participation. Unexpectedly, all three groups were strikingly alike in regard to voting, discussion of politics, and interest in political affairs. A majority of the men in all three groups reported talking politics at least sometimes. Only one man indicated he was not interested in presidential elections. Only a handful felt that the outcome of the 1960 presidential election made no difference. All of the men said they had voted in 1960.

Only in two areas did any tentative difference appear among the three work groups. First, the skilled workers were more likely than the other groups to participate in political activities beyond

---

is some unofficial, quasi-conspiratorial group behind the scenes to manipulate and control public affairs; (2) each cabal group is responsible to no one but itself, and (3) the cabalist argument is protean; for the same person it will focus now upon the international banker and now upon the Communists. . . .

Lane argues that such a pattern of thought is rooted both in personality weaknesses and the social processes of modern society. He finds this frame of mind among men with anti-democratic tendencies. See his *Political Ideology*, ch. 7.

voting. Two-thirds of the skilled group had contributed money, gone to party meetings or actively campaigned in recent years. In the repair group, the figure was 43 per cent, and in the line group, 36 per cent.

Second, the quality of partisan commitment varies considerably among these groups. Very crudely, there are two sorts of commitment: positive and negative—being in favor of, or being against. Most notably, the line workers phrase their political commitments in terms of their aversion for the Republican Party as well as their preference for the Democrats. Five of the twelve line workers speak of their ill-feeling toward the GOP. This ill-feeling runs the gamut from quiet discontent to raw bitterness. Dolski, a line worker, speaks with particular resentment on the subject of poverty: "Why do we have poor people in this state? I'll tell you: Republicans got in there. They kept everything for themselves. Now we got the poor in. . . ."

V

Much of the evidence set out in the preceding sections is impressionistic and statistically insignificant. Yet the weight of the evidence points in a single direction.

It is clear that the two groups of semi-skilled auto workers hold different views in various areas of life. First, the men who work on repetitive, assembly-line jobs dislike their work more and are more hostile toward and alienated from the union. Second, the assembly-line workers are more fatalistic, less sympathetic with and tolerant of others. The line workers are also more radical in their political views.

Recent investigations of Arthur Kornhauser tend to confirm these findings. In an as yet unpublished work and in a recent article, Kornhauser explores the relationships between skill level and various psychological and attitude variables. He finds that skill level in manual jobs is clearly related to mental health and also to certain political and social attitudes. He concludes that the higher the skill level of the job, the more likely that men will show high mental

173

health, while mental health is lowest among workers with repetitive conveyor-paced jobs.[19]

Kornhauser's measures of mental health coincide, in part, with dimensions of attitudes also examined in this study. His indices include measures of: anxiety and tension; hostility *versus* trust in people; self-esteem *versus* negative self-feelings; sociability *versus* withdrawal; personal morale *versus* anomie or social alienation. He also found, consistent with the findings here, that workers in lower skill jobs were higher on economic "liberalism," but lower in liberal attitudes on race relations and international affairs. Kornhauser concludes that the workers at various skill levels differ most sharply in feelings of defeat, pessimism, personal inadequacy, futility, and distrust of others.[20]

---

[19]Arthur Kornhauser, "The Mental Health of the Industrial Worker— A Detroit Study" (preliminary draft, August, 1962); "Mental Health of Factory Workers: A Detroit Study," *Human Organization,* Vol. 21 (1962), pp. 43–46. The following table (*ibid.,* p. 45) will indicate his findings:

MENTAL HEALTH OF FACTORY WORKERS

Men in 40s (age)	% With good mental health scores	N
Skilled	56	45
High Semi-Skilled	41	98
Ordinary SS	38	82
Repetitive SS	26	73
Repetitive machine-paced only (subdivision of preceding category)	16	32

These relationships held when the author controlled for education.

[20]Though I have spoken of a causal relationship between jobs and attitudes, I have not really "proven" such a relationship exists. The crucial problem is one of pre-selection. Perhaps men on assembly-line jobs differ from other semi-skilled workers because they were different before they ever took these jobs, rather than because they have been changed by their employment. Perhaps it is only men with a low sense of self-esteem and

Assembly-line workers, as we have seen, do not find their work interesting. They complain bitterly and consistently about monotony. In many respects, automobile assembly-line work reflects the most unhealthy characteristics of industrial work. Line workers have a sense of futility. They are frustrated and at the same time are seeking to undo their sense of inadequacy. Their frustrations are clearly reflected in their alienation, *i.e.*, their feelings of powerlessness, and its attendant consequences. Their feelings of helplessness are reflected in their fatalistic acceptance of their lot and of the agonies of the great world. Their efforts to restore their self-esteem are reflected in their desires for economic improvement.[21]

What are the implications of these findings for our understanding of political life?

First, it seems reasonable to suppose that assembly-line workers and others whose jobs deprive them of control over their physical movements are more likely to sympathize with radical and mass agitations. Assembly-line workers are more isolated and more likely to feel disenfranchised than other industrial workers. Their feelings about politics are likely to be influenced by desires for relatively radical change, even if these feelings are partly suppressed.

Second, it seems clear that the job structure of industry is one factor that needs to be understood in grasping the impact of industrialization. Kornhauser has pointed out that it is not industrialization *per se*, but rather "discontinuities" in industrial development

---

strong withdrawal tendencies who stay on the assembly-line. Kornhauser tries to handle this problem by exploring the life of his interviewees before they took their present jobs. He concludes that there is demonstrable evidence that jobs change attitudes, regardless of what those attitudes were before the job was taken. If so, then personality differences that exist before taking the job do not explain occupational group differences in mental health. See "Mental Health of Factory Workers," *loc. cit.*, p. 46.

[21]Demands for justice and self-esteem can take many forms. For a discussion see Denis Butt, "Workers' Control," *New Left Review*, No. 10 (July–August 1961), pp. 24–33.

that have been the basis for antidemocratic movements.[22] Among these discontinuities are excessive rapidity of industrialization or the acute breakdown of the economy. Perhaps along with these factors we should also turn our attention to the job structure of emerging industries, focusing on the proportion of assembly-line type jobs.

Third, specific job groups may show a clearer relationship to political party allegiance in countries with multi-party systems than they seem to in America. The great majority of workers in all of the sample groups examined here were Democrats, yet the groups differed in the extent to which they favored liberal economic measures, and in the intensity of their antagonism to the Republicans. In a country where a greater variety of political choices is offered, such differences within the strata of manual workers may show up more sharply in party allegiances. And conversely, if most of the men in most circumstances vote Democratic anyway, regardless of differences in their feelings, party organizers here may well be content to get them to the polls and ignore their feelings.

Finally, how widely can these findings be generalized? If recent work in industrial psychology is any indication, a large percentage of manual and white collar workers are not interested in their work. It seems as yet an open question whether interest in work and control over work will increase or decrease with the spread of various forms of automation. At any rate, millions, if not tens of millions of Americans in the foreseeable future are likely to be working at uninteresting, repetitive jobs. Perhaps such workers, even if they are not manual workers, will internalize the tensions and dissatisfactions of their work.

I am not attempting to argue that a bored clerk in a department store, a dish-washer in a restaurant, an auto assembly worker, and an IBM card puncher are likely to respond to their jobs in the same manner. Their political and social attitudes are conditioned by the content and status of their jobs, as well as the circumstances and expectations they bring with them, and other factors. Yet it seems possible that at each status level, those with the most repetitive, least interesting or controllable

[22]Kornhauser, *The Politics of Mass Society, op. cit.*

jobs will be the most dissatisfied, alienated, and politically "radical."[23]

VI

Various political analysts have argued that there is a causal connection between industrialization and democracy. Among the most prominent of these probably is Lipset, who has shown correlations between stable democratic systems and various indices which provide a way of measuring the relative modernity of nations.[24] In his view, contradicting Marx, industrialization tends to produce the preconditions for political democracy because the class struggle is shaped in moderate directions. Relative wealth and increased education tend to preclude extremism in the lower classes. The absence of deep and stable class differences also makes it possible for the rich and privileged to acknowledge the poor as members of the same species.

Robert Lane has recently buttressed Lipset's argument from another direction. His research, in depth interviews, of the attitudes of a sample of "common men" in an Eastern city reveals that the work situation in which these men find themselves is conducive to the formation of democratic norms. Most of his sample have substantial independence at work, find satisfaction in their jobs, exercise some skill, are in a position to assert their competence and to exchange views with co-workers and superiors. Lane's findings also move in the direction of substantiating Blauner's hypothesis that modern industrial work provides wider opportunities for the exer-

[23]There is an extreme divergence of views concerning the composition of the manual workforce. For example, compare the emphasis in the appendix to Friedmann's *Anatomy of Work—Labor, Leisure and the Implications of Automation*, trans. Wyatt Rawson (New York, 1961), with the notes to Blauner, *loc. cit.*

[24]"Some Social Requisites of Democracy," *American Political Science Review*, Vol. 53 (March 1959), pp. 69–105; see also his *Political Man, op. cit.*, ch. 2.

cise of skill than work in previous societies. Lane concludes that the data on industrial work substantiate Lipset's correlation between democracy and advanced industrial development.[25]

The findings reported here, as well as those of Kornhauser noted above, are not nearly so optimistic as Lane's or Blauner's. It seems that at some lower skill levels work alienation is considerable, and has serious psychological and political consequences, some of which are not very healthy for a democratic polity. On the basis of the very incomplete knowledge we have about the effects of different types of work, skepticism about the overall consequences of industrial work is still in order.

The manual workers examined in this study are not extremists in the sense of favoring truly radical change, revolution, violence, or of lending support to undemocratic political movements. But it is not their jobs, at least in the case of the two groups of semi-skilled workers, that have made them supporters of the *status quo,* nor taught them very much about the nature of democratic social relationships. If these men are defenders of the political *status quo* it seems to be largely because of their status as consumers, not because of their work lives. If they have very much sense of personal adequacy, it is because of the control and judgment they are able to exercise outside their jobs. Though industrial work, for many reasons, may be more conducive to the development of democratic sentiments than the life of the peasant, it is quite another thing to argue that industrial work, at least of the repetitive variety, is generally healthy or enhances an individual's sense of worth.

Lipset's argument concerning the relationship between industrialization and democracy seems to run counter to the analyses of writers such as C. Wright Mills and Erich Fromm. Fromm and Mills emphasize the alienation and apathy characteristic of bureaucratized industrial societies.[26] They argue that democracy is far from

[25]*Political Ideology,* ch. 15.

[26]Mills' point of view is set out in *White Collar, The American Middle Classes* (New York, Oxford Univ. Press, 1951); *The Power Elite* (New York,

being a reality in today's world. As they picture it, many ordinary citizens have become passive and alienated, feel unable to control their fates, and have lost sight of the significant issues of political life. Both Mills and Fromm relate these characteristics of industrial societies to the structure of work. Both argue that alienation and passivity at work breed alienation and passivity elsewhere. If they are right and industrialization creates many kinds of work situations which are not conducive to the development of democratic attitudes, then how can industrialization and democracy be related?

A great part of the difficulty in resolving this antithesis may lie in definitions and points of view. Lipset's definition of democracy is an arbitrary, operational one. He speaks of two characteristics: competitive parties and the absence of strong anti-democratic political groups.[27] It is a "democracy" fitting this definition which Lipset finds related to his indices of modernity. Both Fromm and Mills speak of democracy and democratic attitudes in a different sense. Both bring normative judgments to bear on present reality. So, it is possible to agree that Lipset's correlation is correct and important, and yet to agree with Mills and Fromm that present-day democracies are not as democratic as they might be.

Robert Lane has argued that ego strength is a crucial psychological correlate of democracy. Without having experienced an inner sense of mastery as well as a sense of mastery over the environment, men do not develop the requisite ego strength to pursue a consistent, long-term course, or to effect much social change. One of the most important, if unproven, implications of this study is that the work men do can have important consequences for their ego strength. Here the concerns of Fromm and Mills are significant. Men in a work environment they cannot control may be to some unknown degree damaged in their sense of mastery, and this dam-

---

Oxford Univ. Press, 1959), and *The Causes of World War III* (New York, 1960). Fromm's views can be found, in part, in *The Sane Society* (New York, 1955).

[27] *Political Man*, p. 48.

age may render them less capable of coping with and altering an environment they find unsatisfactory. To the extent that such damage occurs, men become victims rather than creators. To the extent that work life contributes to such incapacities, it needs improvement in modern societies. Industrial democracy may yet prove to be a prerequisite to political and social democracy.

A few final *caveats:* first, the severe dissatisfactions found among automobile assembly-line workers are probably not typical of the attitudes of most modern industrial workers. The nature of the assembly-line itself intensifies the problems of a mechanized job. These findings therefore represent only one segment of the working class. Their relevance to men in other types of jobs which are less intensely disliked remains to be seen.[28] Second, the findings presented in the tables above are for the most part based on a rather crude dichotomizing of attitudes as these attitudes appeared in the setting of open-ended interviews. Such findings, especially in view of the small size of the sample, are at best suggestive and exploratory. Most important, the question of the intensity with which various attitudes are held must remain moot in many of the areas this article has explored. For example, though many of the men criticize what they consider to be manipulative practices by political figures, most of them are not "alienated" from the political system. How deep their cynicism may go on occasion, is a question this study has not touched.[29]

[28]For a comparison of "alienation" in several quite different industrial settings, see Robert Blauner, *Alienation and Freedom* (Chicago, 1964).

[29]Allen Schick provides a perceptive discussion of the need to deal realistically with the presence of ambivalent political attitudes in his paper, "Alienation and Politics," delivered at the 1964 American Political Science Association convention.

APPENDIX B

PATHWAYS TO PARTICIPATION*

PAUL ALLEN BECK
Florida State University

M. KENT JENNINGS
University of California, Santa Barbara;
University of Michigan, Ann Arbor

*We have selected excerpts from this article in order to illustrate the applications of regression analysis. The complete article may be found in *The American Political Science Review*, Vol. 76, No. 1 (March, 1982), pp. 94–108. We thank the authors, Paul Allen Beck and M. Kent Jennings, for their permission to reprint these excerpts.

APPENDIX B

The premise of this article is that adult participation in politics is affected by strong preadult forces in addition to the contemporaneous factors emphasized by recent studies. To test this premise, data are drawn from the 1965–1973 national socialization panel study of young Americans and their parents. Four causal models depicting pathways to participation among young adults are evaluated; each includes civic orientations as intervening variables. Three of the models assess the direct and indirect effects of parental characteristics—socioeconomic status, political activity, and civic orientations. The fourth model assesses the impact of adolescent involvement in high school activities. Taken individually, each pathway is shown to have an effect on adult participation, with parent socioeconomic status and high school activism having the most impact. When the four pathways are combined in a single model to reflect the connections among them, all remain important. The combined model illustrates the importance of a variety of methods of political learning. The combined model also demonstrates the crucial role of civic orientations in converting preadult experiences into later participation. Civic orientations are the primary carriers of preadult political learning. Overall, the results rebut the critics of socialization research who have questioned the existence of a linkage between early learning and adult political behavior.

. . . One area in which preadult political socialization may influence adult political behavior is political participation. Research on participation has been dominated to date by perspectives drawn from analysis of cross-sectional data. The pioneering work of Verba and Nie (1972) follows this approach in its emphasis on contemporaneous factors—e.g., social status, civic attitudes, organizational involvement, group consciousness, and age—to explain participation. Milbrath and Goel's (1977) survey of the determinants of participation adopts the same approach and illustrates even more fully the dependence of participation research on correlations between activity and contemporary factors.

This approach neglects important alternative explanations for political participation, especially those in which current participative behavior is viewed as a product of preadult political learning. Viewing political participation from a socialization perspective offers the possibility of detecting preadult structuring for an important form of political behavior, which supports one key assumption in political socialization research and broadens our understanding of the determinants of participation.

Here we adopt the longitudinal perspective necessary to specify the effects of preadult socialization on adult political activity. Knowledge of the orientations and behavior of young adults during their adolescence eight years before, and those of their parents at that time, enables us to estimate pathways to young adult participation through the socialization process. In particular, we shall evaluate the contributions to the political participation of young adults that stem from parent socioeconomic status, parent political participation, parent civic orientations when the child was still in the home, and the young adult's participation in high school activities eight years earlier.

The data base for this analysis is a two-wave panel study of young Americans and their parents. The first wave is a representative cross-section sample of high school seniors and their parents, personally interviewed in the spring of 1965. The second wave, conducted in early 1973, consists of personal interviews with 1,119 of the youths and 1,118 of their parents as well as mail questionnaires for 229 youths and 61 parents.[1] Our attention is restricted to the 1,272 parent-child cases containing observations of the youths at each time and of the parents in 1965. For convenience we will

---

[1] The study was conducted by the Center for Political Studies at the University of Michigan under the direction of M. Kent Jennings. The 1965 youth and parent samples represent the populations of 1965 high school seniors and their parents, respectively. Reinterview rates of 81 percent for the youths and 75 percent for the parents, as well as insubstantial differences in 1965 characteristics between those reinterviewed and not reinterviewed in 1973 (see Jennings and Niemi, 1981, Appendix A), assure us that the 1973 samples represent these same populations well eight years later. The data are now available through the Inter-University Consortium for Political and Social Research (study number 7779).

refer to the "children" in 1965 as youths or adolescents and in 1973 as young adults.

These data are well suited for examining, in longitudinal fashion, the contributions of childhood socialization to young adult participation. They allow direct measurement of important factors in the socialization process: the attitudes and behavior of parents when the child was still in the home and of the children as late adolescents. These materials also embrace virtually the full range of significant participation for young adults as they aged from 17–18 to 25–26. Finally, the data contain extensive information on the young adults in 1973.

The political participation measure used in the study is an additive index based on nine different activities. Five of these reflect involvement in election campaigns from 1965 to 1973, including referenda and contests for public office at all levels, by means of persuading others how to vote, attending meetings or rallies, displaying buttons or bumper stickers, donating money, and doing any other type of campaign work. The four remaining items cover nonelectoral activities performed at any previous time: writing letters to the editor, contacting public officials, engaging in protests or demonstrations, and working with others to solve community problems. Although these activities represent several different modes of participation, they are sufficiently similar to be combined into a unidimensional index of political activity[2]. . . .

The Intergenerational SES Model

Several decades of empirical research have established socioeconomic status as a major determinant of political participation. Higher-status people have been found to be more active in politics than lower-status people regardless of how status is measured (Milbrath and Goel, 1977) or of the political system under study, except where

---

[2]All nine activities were intercorrelated substantially with one another ($r > .35$) and loaded well ($> .35$) on the first factor in a principal component factor analysis. See Beck and Jennings (1979) for an extensive discussion of the construction of this measure.

political conditions lead to the mobilization of low-status groups (Nie, Powell, and Prewitt, 1969; Verba, Nie, and Kim, 1978). Status differentials in participation seem the normal condition of political life.

Although attributes of status per se may facilitate participation, it is generally conceded that status represents factors tied more directly to activism. Verba and Nie (1972) identify civic orientations as the most important of these factors. Civic orientations increase the psychological benefits of and the attitudinal resources for participation. Civic orientations in turn are thought to be strongly influenced by socioeconomic status, especially education. Although these orientations cannot account fully for the empirical relationship between status and participation, they explain a sizable portion of it.

An SES model of political activity, with civic orientations as mediating variables, is employed by Verba and Nie (1972) as the primary predictor of participation and as a baseline against which to gauge the effects of other factors. After the Verba and Nie study, what they titled "the standard SES model" stood as the foremost explanatory model of participation. . . .

This analysis establishes the *intermediate* role of the standard SES model in explaining political activity. Neither socioeconomic status nor civic orientations spring to life upon attainment of adulthood. Rather, the roots of both lie in parent socioeconomic status and the economic, social, psychological, and political resources for later life that it provides. This requires some revision in interpretations of the standard SES model. In particular, these interpretations must recognize that political orientations develop prior to the attainment of adult socioeconomic status and that this fact raises serious questions about the impact of the respondent's own status. The standard SES model is only the most recent chapter in the story of the development of adult political participation.

The Parent Civic Orientations Model

The intergenerational SES model describes a pathway to participation that is nonpolitical in nature. An alternative approach to parental influence, potentially as rewarding in explaining why adults participate in politics, is to focus attention on explicitly political characteristics of parents and preadult family life.

185

APPENDIX B

The seeds for later participation may be sown directly through the process of *political* socialization with parents playing the leading role. The participation of young adults is linked to their civic orientations. These civic orientations may be as much the legacy of childhood political socialization as the products of socioeconomic status. Parental political involvement and civic competence may be transmitted to offspring through traditional socialization mechanisms. In particular, highly politicized parents may foster a family atmosphere charged with positive civic orientations, thus endowing their children with the motivational prerequisites for later participation. In sum, one pathway to participation may lie through the intergenerational transfer of political attitudes.

These theoretical expectations are formalized in the parent civic orientations model presented in Figure B.1. The measure of parent civic orientations in this model combines political interest, political knowledge, and the subjective competence component of political efficacy (see Footnote 3). Parent data are from 1965, when the child lived in the home.

The estimates for this model show that parent civic orientations influence significantly the participation of children as young adults eight years later. Parental outlooks apparently leave a lasting impression that can be translated later into political activity. This influence is largely indirect. Parent civic orientations in 1965 were related to the orientations of their children as high school seniors in the same year. In turn, these childhood orientations contributed to subsequent political activity, both directly and through young adult civic orientations. The most important compound path is the longest: from parents through youth orientations to young adult orientations then on to participation. Parent civic orientations also enjoyed a significant direct, or unmediated, impact on young adult political activities.

These results trace the roots of adult political activity to the child's political world—before the citizen's involvement in the adult world of politics. The primary influence here can be attributed to parents, long considered the foremost agents of political socialization (Beck, 1977). That influence, furthermore, seems to be carried by explicitly political orientations—the first indication in our study that *political* socialization structures subsequent adult behavior.

186

FIGURE B.1. THE PARENT CIVIC ORIENTATIONS MODEL*

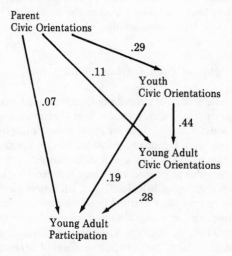

SOURCE: 1965–73 Parent-Child Socialization Panel, Center for Political Studies, University of Michigan.

*Entries are the standardized regression or path coefficients estimated for the model depicted by the arrows. Solid lines indicate significance at the .01 level. Dashed lines indicate an estimated path coefficient that was insignificant. Residual path coefficients are not shown. The R^2 of young adult participation on all predictor variables is .19.

Effects of Parent Civic Orientations

Direct = .07
Indirect (through youth civic orientations) = .06
Indirect (through young adult civic orientations) = .07
Total = .07 + .06 + .07 = .20

Our data cannot reveal the mechanisms through which parental orientations toward civic involvement influence their offspring, but we can picture how this might occur. Parent civic orientations may set the tone of family discourse on politics. Parent interest probably promotes discussion of politics in the home, awakening the child's interest in the world of politics. Parent political knowledge can enhance the child's own understanding of politics in these

187

discussions. Less cognitively based orientations, such as political efficacy, probably are transmitted less consciously by parents, but they are no less likely to be included in the attitudinal baggage the young carry with them into adulthood.

The Parent Political Participation Model

Another possible source of parent political influence is parent political involvement itself. Through the mechanism of imitation, the offspring of activists may adopt an activist stance themselves. Biographical accounts of famous political leaders and period pieces on student radicals in the youth generation (Keniston, 1968) are replete with examples of people who have followed in their parents' footsteps by becoming political activists. Imitation surely is not the only mechanism operating in these families. Parent political activity may affect children's attitudes about politics and consequently their participation. Thus, there is good reason to build civic orientations into this model too, in order to capture effects of parental participation that may be mediated through the child's orientations toward political life.

These theoretical expectations are assessed in the parent political participation model presented in Figure B.2. Parent participation is measured by the number of campaign activities performed by the parent.[3] Although the measure is restricted to only one of three recognized dimensions of nonelectoral political activity, making it narrower than that for the young adults, the campaign activities dimension is highly representative of political participation in

---

[3]The six campaign activities are attempting to influence others, attending rallies, belonging to political clubs, using campaign buttons or stickers, donating money, and performing any other campaign-related activities. These activities are significantly intercorrelated ($r \geqslant .24$) and fall on the first dimension (loadings $\geqslant .52$) of a principal component factor analysis. As a result they can be combined into a single measure. Unfortunately, information on noncampaign participation was not collected for the parents in 1965.

general. It was strongly correlated ($r = .88$) with overall participation in the Verba and Nie study (1972, p. 75).

The path coefficients for this model provide evidence of substantial parent contributions to young adult political activity through the parents' own political participation. The direct effects are twice the indirect effects, suggesting that pure imitation with-

FIGURE B.2. THE PARENT POLITICAL PARTICIPATION MODEL*

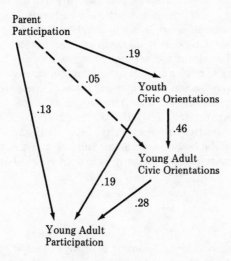

SOURCE: 1965–73 Parent-Child Socialization Panel, Center for Political Studies, University of Michigan.

*Entries are the standardized regression or path coefficients estimated for the model depicted by the arrows. Solid lines indicate significance at the .01 level. Dashed lines indicate an estimated path coefficient that was insignificant. Residual path coefficients are not shown. The R^2 of young adult participation on all predictor variables is .20.

Effects of Parent Participation

Direct = .13
Indirect (through civic orientations) = .07
Total = .13 + .07 = .20

out an attitudinal boost is a powerful socialization force in this case. Yet parent participation does exert some indirect impact on young adult activity by stimulating the development of civic orientations. Interestingly, the indirect effects are slightly stronger when relayed through youth civic orientations rather than through the contemporaneous young adult orientations. These relationships, however, are of modest strength. Parents are often active without any apparent impact on child civic orientations, and children develop positive civic orientations in the absence of parent participation.

The parent political participation model contributes to an understanding of young adult political activity, rivaling the parent civic orientation model in total effects. Neither is as successful, though, as the parent socioeconomic status model. One reason is that their key variables are not gauged as well as is status. For one thing, the participation or civic orientations of one parent may not reflect the levels of the other (Jennings and Niemi, 1971; Niemi, Newman, and Weimer, 1981). By contrast, parent SES is shared by both parents, particularly since it has been measured by the status of the head of the household. The measure of status, education, also surely is more reliable than the measures of political attitudes and activity. . . .

Conclusion

We have evaluated four different pathways to adult participation that originate in the preadult years. Taken individually, each is shown to influence adult participation. This influence persists even when interdependencies among the four models are taken into account. Parent socioeconomic status, parent participation, youth high school activity, and parent civic orientations all make distinct contributions to young adult political participation. For parent status and parent civic orientations, the influence is largely indirect. For parent participation and high school activity, it is almost entirely direct.

These results demonstrate that political activity is a consequence of noncontemporaneous forces, signifying the importance of the political socialization process. Through a variety of socialization mechanisms, parents and schools leave a legacy for later participation profiles. While it may be reflected in adult characteristics, this legacy is established long before adult characteristics have formed. To be sure, contemporaneous adult characteristics remain important predictors of participation. All that our results require is that socialization influences be considered along with them if we are to explain political participation adequately.

These results have interesting implications for the biases of political participation. It is well established that the activists in American politics "sing with a strong upper-class accent," to quote Schattschneider's (1960, p. 35) famous metaphor. While the results of our study hardly dispute this point, they also uncover alternative paths to participation that bypass status. Some forces in the home and school operate to counteract the socioeconomic status bias of participation—forces which themselves are only weakly related to SES. If the operations of these forces are imperiled or become dependent upon status, however, the SES bias of participation will be accentuated. Seen in this light, restricted opportunities for high school extracurricular activity or a weakening of partisan and material inducements for participation among parents can limit the chances for nonstatus based participation in the next generation.

Most importantly, the findings of this study lend strong support to the premise that preadult socialization affects adult attitudes and behavior. Challenges to this premise have survived in part because of the absence of data linking preadulthood to adulthood among the same individuals. Armed with such evidence, we have shown that the challenge can be rebutted in the domain of political participation. At least for young adults in the late 1960s and early 1970s, political activity was *structured* to a significant degree by the socialization process. If such an effect appears here, it may appear for other attitudes and behaviors as well. Perhaps a search for the effects of preadult political socialization can refocus the field of political socialization and consequently increase our understanding of the wellspring of adult political attitudes and behavior.

References

Almond, Gabriel, and Sidney Verba (1963). *The Civic Culture*. Princeton, N.J.: Princeton University Press.

APPENDIX B

Balch, George (1974). "Multiple Indicators in Survey Research: The Concept 'Sense of Political Efficacy'." *Political Methodology* 1:1–43.

Beck, Paul Allen (1977). "The Role of Agents in Political Socialization." In Stanley Allen Renshon (ed.), *Handbook of Political Socialization*. New York: The Free Press, pp. 115–142.

Beck, Paul Allen, and M. Kent Jennings (1979). "Political Periods and Political Participation." *American Political Science Review* 73: 737–751.

Blau, Peter, and Otis D. Duncan (1968). *The American Occupational Structure*. New York: Wiley.

Clarke, James W., and Henry C. Kenski (1974). "Communication." *American Political Science Review* 68: 722–725.

Connell, R. W. (1972). "Political Socialization in the American Family: The Evidence Re-Examined." *Public Opinion Quarterly* 36: 323–333.

Dawson, Richard E., Kenneth Prewitt, and Karen S. Dawson (1977). *Political Socialization*. Boston: Little, Brown.

Easton, David, and Jack Dennis (1967). "The Child's Acquisition of Regime Norms: Political Efficacy." *American Political Science Review* 61: 25–38.

Ehman, Lee H. (1969). "An Analysis of the Relationship of Selected Educational Variables with the Political Socialization of High School Students." *American Educational Research Journal* 4: 559–580.

Featherman, David L., and Robert M. Hauser (1978). *Opportunity and Change*. New York: Academic Press.

Greenstein, Fred I. (1974). "Communication." *American Political Science Review* 68: 720–722.

Hess, Robert D., and Judith V. Torney (1967). *The Development of Political Attitudes in Children*. Chicago: Aldine.

Jennings, M. Kent (1980). "Comment on Richard Merelman's 'Democratic Politics and the Culture of American Education'." *American Political Science Review* 74: 333–337.

Jennings, M. Kent, Kenneth P. Langton, and Richard G. Niemi (1974). "Effects of the High School Civics Curriculum." In M. Kent Jennings and Richard G. Niemi, *The Political Character of Adolescence*. Princeton, N.J.: Princeton University Press, Chapter 7.

Jennings, M. Kent, and Richard G. Niemi (1971). "The Division of Political Labor Between Mothers and Fathers." *American Political Science Review* 65: 69–82.

Jennings, M. Kent, and Richard G. Niemi (1981). *Generations and Politics*. Princeton, N.J.: Princeton University Press.

Keniston, Kenneth (1968). *Young Radicals*. New York: Harcourt, Brace, and World.

Lipset, Seymour Martin (1960). *Political Man.* Garden City, N.Y.: Double-day.

Marsh, David (1971). "Political Socialization: The Implicit Assumptions Questioned." *British Journal of Political Science* 1: 453–465.

Merelman, Richard M. (1980). "Democratic Politics and the Culture of American Education." *American Political Science Review* 74: 319–332.

Milbrath, Lester W., and M. Lal Goel (1977). *Political Participation.* Chicago: Rand McNally.

Nie, Norman H., Bingham Powell, and Kenneth Prewitt (1969). "Social Structure and Political Participation." *American Political Science Review* 63: 361–378 and 808–832.

Niemi, Richard G., David Newman, and David L. Weimer (1981). "Reassessing the Political Influence of Parents on Children." Unpublished manuscript.

Rapoport, Ronald B. (1981). "The Sex Gap in Political Persuading: Where the 'Structuring Principle' Works." *American Journal of Political Science* 25: 32–48.

Schattschneider, E. E. (1960). *The Semisovereign People.* Hinsdale: Ill.: The Dryden Press.

Searing, Donald, and Joel Schwartz (1974). "Communication." *American Political Science Review* 68: 725–729.

Searing, Donald, Joel J. Schwartz, and Alden E. Lind (1973). "The Structuring Principle: Political Socialization and Belief Systems." *American Political Science Review* 67: 415–432.

Searing, Donald, Gerald Wright, and George Rabinowitz (1976). "The Primacy Principle: Attitude Change and Political Socialization." *British Journal of Political Science* 6: 83–113.

Sigel, Roberta, and Marilyn Hoskins (1981). *The Political Involvement of Adolescents.* New Brunswick, N.J.: Rutgers University Press.

Verba, Sidney, and Norman H. Nie (1972). *Participation in America.* New York: Harper & Row.

Verba, Sidney, Norman H. Nie, and Jae-on Kim (1978). *Participation and Political Equality.* Cambridge, England: Cambridge University Press.

Ziblatt, David (1965). "High School Extracurricular Activities and Political Socialization." *The Annals of the American Academy of Political and Social Science* 361: 20–31.

INDEX

195

INDEX

INDEX